D0122096

*A Nation of Laws*

# A Nation of Laws

## America's Imperfect Pursuit

## of Justice

Peter Charles Hoffer

*University Press of Kansas*

Published by the University Press of Kansas (Lawrence, Kansas 66045), which
was organized by the Kansas Board of Regents and is operated and funded by
Emporia State University, Fort Hays State University, Kansas State University,
Pittsburg State University, the University of Kansas, and Wichita State
University

Library of Congress Cataloging-in-Publication Data

Hoffer, Peter Charles, 1944–
A nation of laws : America's imperfect pursuit of justice / Peter Charles Hoffer.
p. cm.
Includes bibliographical references and index.
ISBN 978-0-7006-1707-4 (cloth : alk. paper)
1. Law–United States–History. I. Title.
KF352.H64 2010
349.73˙DC22
2009052159

British Library Cataloguing-in-Publication Data is available.

Printed in the United States of America

10 9 8 7 6 5 4 3 2 1

The paper used in this publication is recycled and contains 30 percent
postconsumer waste. It is acid free and meets the minimum requirements of
the American National Standard for Permanence of Paper for Printed Library
Materials Z39.48-1992.

*For Stephen Botein, classmate and friend,*
*and Kermit Hall, mentor and patron.*
*They are greatly missed.*

# Contents

*Acknowledgments*

Acknowledgments are always in order. I first taught American legal history in 1983. I am grateful to my then colleague Michal Belknap for his support and to my lifetime collaborator N. E. H. Hull for continuing inspiration. Early on, Kermit Hall and Stephen Botein helped shape my teaching. A year at Harvard Law School and course work with Abe Chayes, Terry Fisher, Mort Horwitz, Lew Sargentish, and Cass Sunstein honed my thinking. Conversations about legal history with Les Benedict, Harold Hyman, and Stan Katz were valuable. In the fall of 1992, Mike Briggs of the University Press of Kansas asked if UPK should publish a legal history series. That offer resulted in the Landmark Law Cases and American Society series, which I coedit, and further opportunity to work with other scholars in history, law, and political science. The effort here gained greatly from comments by Richard Bernstein, Al Brophy, Lawrence Friedman, and Stan Katz. Williamjames Hoffer and N. E. H. Hull give new meaning to the term "in house" reading of manuscripts. They are coauthors of other projects as well. Collaboration with them makes the entire enterprise of scholarship a delight. Mike Briggs still graces UPK with his now legendary warmth, good sense, and decency. He is a super editor-in-chief. Assistant director Susan Schott wrote that she was "jazzed" by the prospect of marketing the book, and coming from flat out the best marketing director in the business that is just what any author wants to hear. My thanks to all of them, and to you for opening the book. Enjoy!

# Introduction:
## A Nation of Laws

On May 21, 2009, President Barack Obama spoke to the American people about the continuing threat of terrorist activity. He promised that the government would remain vigilant, but he added,

> My own American journey was paved by generations of citizens who gave meaning to those simple words—"to form a more perfect union." I've studied the Constitution as a student, I've taught it as a teacher, I've been bound by it as a lawyer and a legislator. I took an oath to preserve, protect, and defend the Constitution as Commander-in-Chief, and as a citizen, I know that we must never, ever, turn our back on its enduring principles for expedience sake.

The president, a lawyer and the foremost law officer in the land, reminded his fellow Americans that "we are a nation of laws."[1]

The ideal that President Obama held aloft goes back to the founding fathers. They, too, extolled a nation of laws, for only a settled law, fairly enforced, could protect liberty and property in the new republic against corruption and tyranny. As John Adams in retirement recalled his response to British depreda-

tions on American liberties in the midst of the revolutionary crisis, "is this the conduct of a good judicial character in a free
country, and under a government of laws"? The answer was as
plain to him in 1816, when he penned his recollection, as in
1776, when he voted for independence. The ideal was "good
laws, and such as were well calculated for the support of liberty."[2]

Adams's and Obama's professed faith that we are a nation
of laws is reassuring in a world of lawless terrorism. Our leaders
should adhere to this doctrine. But lest we adopt a self-satisfied
or celebratory view of our legal history, we should return to the
historical moments to which Adams and Obama referred. The
controversies that led to the American Revolution were primarily legal, a bare-knuckled resistance to the imposition of parliamentary regulations in the colonies. Lawyers on both sides
traded blows. Did Americans have a legal right to their property
and persons or were these privileges that the crown could
rescind at will? To vindicate those claims of rights, Adams and
the other revolutionaries violated oaths of obedience to the
crown and supported the violent overthrow of the home government.

When Obama spoke to the nation, he conceded the illegal
means and methods his predecessors had adopted to counter
suspected domestic terrorism. "Faced with an uncertain threat,
our government made a series of hasty decisions." Obama admitted that those decisions violated our own and international law.
They "failed to rely on our legal traditions and time-tested institutions." He promised that "my administration has begun to
reshape the standards that apply to ensure that they are in line
with the rule of law," but in fact he did not jettison all of the
extra-constitutional expediencies of the former administration.[3]

It is true that the law in America has always been the foundation of a way of life. From the inception of the nation, through
all its travails and triumphs, law has woven its way. Law is the
mark and measure of American democratic republicanism. Its

lawgivers are not an elite aristocracy nor a divinely chosen few. Instead, they are the representatives of the people. Americans are legal actors on a scale unparalleled in history. Much of American law is made by the people themselves when they choose to litigate for their rights. The law belongs in a very personal way to all Americans.

It is also true that most of America's lawmakers are politicians, and they make and interpret law to suit partisan interests and ideologies. As a result, not all Americans have been equal under the law. In our past, some enjoyed all the benefits of citizenship. Some were excluded from many of those benefits. Some were never even accorded the status of persons under the law. The concept of a nation of laws is not self-actuating. It is a contested ideal.

Legal history teaches us that the course of the law in America has not been a linear progress from inequality, privilege, and narrowness of spirit upward toward liberty and dignity for all. Instead, the law has crawled crabwise over the landscape of our history, pulled and driven by competing notions of rights and duties. The result is not a single path of the law, but a multiplicity of paths, some deeply trodden, others ending abruptly, going nowhere. A clear view of our legal history reveals ambiguities and contradictions, quarrels and confrontations. These mirror the struggles within American history itself, for Americans turned to law to resolve conflict. When they did, they etched that conflict on the face of the law. But those controversies allowed many Americans to join or comment in the lawmaking process, reinforcing the central role of law in American life.

*A Nation of Laws* is a collection of interpretive topical essays on our legal history. It introduces the complexities of our laws, the diversity of our lawmakers, and the way in which our law informs events and ideas in our political, economic, and social history. It argues for the vitality of our legal institutions and tracks the failures of our law. Each essay stands on its own. Each addresses the larger question of whether we are a nation of laws, and whether those laws apply to all of us fairly.

Four brief notes complete this introduction. First, this is not a work of jurisprudence. I offer no comprehensive theory of how law works or should work, but it may be useful to note in passing that one school of jurisprudents, called legal positivists, define law as the command of the state that one must obey or face consequences. For other philosophers of law, law is the will of the citizenry that the state embodies in its statutes and judicial decisions. Law that does not fit the values of the community will not be obeyed. The historian of law who finds merit in both of these definitions, as I do, will naturally see a law that sometimes wars with itself.

The second note concerns the boundary between legal history and constitutional history. By a convention lost in the mists of time, historians, political scientists, and jurists divide American legal history into constitutional history and legal history proper. The former focuses on the text of the federal Constitution and the decisions of the U.S. Supreme Court, the latter on the substantive and procedural law and to some extent the conduct of lawyers, legal education, and the legislatures. They are taught in distinct courses and books about them are wary of crossing over some sort of invisible border between them. I believe that constitutional history is a part of legal history. There is no bright line distinction between the two subjects. The High Court is wont to offer its opinion on matters well beyond the scope of the Constitution and the penumbras of the Constitution reach into the farthest corners of everyday legal activity. It is all of a piece and all of it belongs in any introduction to American legal history.

Third, I offer here a particular definition of nation. I do not mean the nation state of the political scientists or the historical geographers. My nation is less fixed in time and place. It is America, and I range in time from the Pilgrims to the present. I hope this somewhat impressionistic sense of nationhood is not untoward. For in truth many of our laws, and surely our ideal of law, predate 1776 or 1787. Some of them came with the Pilgrims and some the Pilgrims found among the native peoples.

The fourth and final note: although terms and concepts of "black letter law" appear throughout this book, it is not a law book. I am interested in historical events and changing ideas of law more than hornbook (legal textbook) detail. But as in the previous sentence, I have tried to give short definitions for "terms of art," words whose meaning in law is not what it is in common parlance. For example, the execution of a writ is not the legally sanctioned murder of a writer, but the delivery of a court order by the appropriate official to the appropriate party to a lawsuit.

# A Nation of Laws

# Prologue:
## Slavery and Race Law

This is the story we would like to tell about a nation of laws: We would like the great ideals of freedom and equality to be not just empty words but concepts anchored in law. We want to believe that "the Constitution and the Bill of Rights . . . stressed rights against the state and other powers. America began and continues as the most anti-statist, legalistic, and rights-oriented nation." As Chief Justice Earl Warren wrote in the companion to *Brown v. Board of Education, Bolling v. Sharpe* (1954), a decision striking down school segregation in the District of Columbia, "our American ideal of fairness" is embodied in concepts like "equal protection and due process" of law.[1]

But this is only half of the story, and it is important to know the rest. For if we are a nation of laws, that law seems to wear two faces. It promotes and it denies; it enables and it punishes; it protects some and not others.

The founders of the American nation believed that the fount of all law should be the sovereignty of "the people." They rejected the monarchical lawgiving of their former colonial masters and substituted for it constitutions based on voter ratification. As Thomas Paine wrote in "Common Sense" (1776), "A government of our own is our natural right." Virginia's Thomas Jefferson captured the spirit of this new legal regime of rights in the Declaration of Independence. He wrote that "We hold these truths to be self-evident, that all men are created equal, that they are endowed by their Creator with certain unalienable Rights, that among these are Life, Liberty and the pursuit of Happiness.—That to secure these rights, Governments are instituted among Men, deriving their just powers from the consent of the governed."[2]

But everyone in the Continental Congress who voted for the Declaration of Independence knew that Jefferson owned slaves, and that slaves, along with women, Catholics, Jews, Indians, and a host of others could not give their consent to the new government because they could not vote. While Jefferson and his fellow committeemen drafted the Declaration, George Mason and other Virginia planters were writing slavery into the state's first constitution. Mason believed devoutly in the notion of human rights and would be one of the authors of the Bill of Rights. Privately Mason called slavery "that slow poison, which is daily contaminating the minds and morals of our people." But when he and his fellow revolutionaries reused the language of the Declaration as a preamble to the state constitution, they added to "all men" the phrase "when in a state of society." They thus consciously excluded slaves, who could not, because they were property, ever be in a state of society. For Jefferson and Mason, the law's two faces were inescapable.[3]

The highest law of the land, the federal Constitution, never mentioned the word "slavery," and that omission was made on purpose to avoid South Carolina and Georgia walking out of the convention, until the Thirteenth Amendment in 1865 made slavery unconstitutional. But slavery could not exist without the protection of law. Without laws friendly to slave owners, their treatment of men and women they enslaved would open them to criminal prosecution for kidnaping, false imprisonment, assault and battery, and perhaps even rape and murder. State law enabled slavery.

The framers of the federal Constitution conceded to the slave states a so-called Three-Fifths Compromise, allowing slave states to count three-fifths of their bondmen and women for the purpose of congressional apportionment, even though the slaves were property, not persons, under state law. The Rendition Clause of Article IV, section 2, "no person held to service or labor in one state, under the laws thereof, escaping to another, shall . . . be discharged from such service or labor, but shall be delivered up, on claim of the party to whom the labor or service is due," patently referred to runaway slaves. In 1793, Congress passed the first Fugitive Slave Act, stating that no state "shall entertain, or give countenance to, the enemies of the other, or protect, in their respective states, criminal fugitives, servants, or slaves, but the same to apprehend and secure, and deliver to the state or states, to which such enemies, criminals, servants, or slaves, respectively belong" providing the enforcement mechanism for the Rendition Clause. A nation of laws accommodated slavery.[4]

Antislavery thought was not a major impulse in America until the nineteenth century, but by the 1830s abolitionists were reading the federal Constitution in the light of the Declaration. Abolitionist legal theorist Lysander Spooner argued that the true and only foundation of law was moral right, a principle of "natural justice" that must mean slavery was illegal. The Constitution, rightly interpreted, in fact the only way that it could be interpreted, was in favor of freedom. "As a legal instrument, there is no trace of slavery in it." The absent word "slavery" could not be reintroduced by statute or judicial interpretation. In *Commonwealth v. Thomas Aves* (1836), Chief Justice Lemuel Shaw of the Massachusetts Superior Judicial Court determined that

each sovereign state, governed by its own laws, although competent and well authorized to make such laws as it

may think most expedient to the extent of its own
territorial limits, and for the government of its own
subjects, yet beyond those limits, and over those who are
not her own subjects, has no authority to enforce her own
laws, or to treat the laws of other states as void, although
contrary to its own views of morality.

In Massachusetts, "the principles of justice, humanity and sound policy, as we adopt them and found our own laws upon them," barred
slavery. Thomas Aves could not keep a slave in Massachusetts.[5]

Could a nation of laws be half slave and half free? Long
before Abraham Lincoln asked a version of that question, a democratic revolution in state constitutionalism had expanded the
franchise greatly. In South Carolina, young state legislator John
C. Calhoun led the effort to drop the property qualification for
voters and soon Carolina allowed all its free white males to vote.
Even as law threw open South Carolina's polls, it continued to
exclude huge segments of its population. African Americans
could not vote in South Carolina, although people of African
ancestry were a majority of South Carolina's population. There,
whether free or enslaved, they had no political identity. As Calhoun explained in 1837,

I take higher ground. I hold that in the present state of
civilization, where two races of different origin, and
distinguished by color, and other physical differences, as
well as intellectual, are brought together, the relation now
existing in the slaveholding States between the two, is,
instead of an evil, a good—a positive good. . . . I hold then,
that there never has yet existed a wealthy and civilized
society in which one portion of the community did not, in
point of fact, live on the labor of the other. Broad and
general as is this assertion, it is fully borne out by history.[6]

Could a nation of laws accommodate such gaping contradictions? U.S. Supreme Court Chief Justice Roger Taney wrote of African Americans in *Dred Scott v. Sanford* (1857),

> It is difficult at this day to realize the state of public opinion in relation to that unfortunate race, which prevailed in the civilized and enlightened portions of the world at the time of the Declaration of Independence, and when the Constitution of the United States was framed and adopted. . . . They had for more than a century before been regarded as beings of an inferior order, and altogether unfit to associate with the white race, either in social or political relations; and so far inferior, that they had no rights which the white man was bound to respect.

Taney believed he spoke not for slaveholders alone, nor for the southern section of the country, but for the law. There was one law for the entire nation, and that law accommodated human bondage.[7]

But Taney's views of the nation's laws were not the only ones the High Court justices expressed. In dissent, Justice John McLean of Ohio read American legal history in an entirely different way from Taney: "It was said that a colored citizen would not be an agreeable member of society. This is more a matter of taste than of law. Several of the States have admitted persons of color to the right of suffrage, and in this view have recognized them as citizens; and this has been done in the slave as well as the free States. . . . They have exercised all the rights of citizens." For Taney and McLean, competing visions of the law existed side by side, reflecting competing legal histories. Both men believed that the nation was bound by law, but they disagreed profoundly about the nature of that law.[8]

Abolitionists who helped runaway slaves escape slave catchers in antebellum America disobeyed the federal Fugitive Slave Laws of 1793 and 1850. These gave to slave catchers, a kind of professional bounty hunter, the legal right to use force to detain a person of color, bring him or her or an entire family before a magistrate, and obtain an order to remove them to the South. The suspected runaway was assumed to be a slave with no legal rights—no right to a jury trial, to confront and cross-examine witnesses, to produce evidence—that the magistrate was required to follow. Northern states resisted these statutes with other enactments called Personal Liberty Laws. These afforded some protection to black citizens of free states, for example the right to a jury trial. Southern congressmen viewed these as illegal. The Supreme Court of the United States agreed with the southern lawgivers, in *Ableman v. Booth* (1859) opining that free states could not interfere with the federal government's protection of southern slave owners' property rights. Taney wrote "No one will suppose that a Government which has now lasted nearly seventy years, enforcing its laws by its own tribunals, and preserving the union of the States, could have lasted a single year, or fulfilled the high trusts committed to it, if offences against its laws could not have been punished without the consent of the State in which the culprit was found."[9]

Perhaps this dichotomy between slavery and freedom poses too stern a test for our query, are we a nation of laws. Surely it posed a stern test for the very existence of the nation. But was the question of slavery not settled by a Civil War and an amendment to the Constitution barring slavery under state or federal law? Yes and no. For although the Thirteenth Amendment ended slavery and the Fourteenth Amendment (1868) mandated that states afford citizens of the United States residing in that state "equal protection" of the law, southern Jim Crow laws invidiously classified people by race and southern state governments refused to protect the rights of African Americans. Law mandated that black Americans accept demeaning and unequal status. In *Plessy v. Ferguson* (1896), the Supreme Court decided that "separate but equal" public facilities, in this case the requirement that people of color ride in railroad cars separate from "white" people, fulfilled this requirement. Justice John Marshall Harlan alone dissented.

> In respect of civil rights, common to all citizens, the Constitution of the United States does not, I think, permit any public authority to know the race of those entitled to be protected in the enjoyment of such rights. . . . Indeed, such legislation, as that here in question, is inconsistent not only with that equality of rights which pertains to citizenship, National and State, but with the personal liberty enjoyed by every one within the United States.[10]

For more than a half century, *Plessy* provided the legal basis for Jim Crow segregation of schools, parks, restaurants, bus stations, and just about every other public space, amusement venue, and government office in the South. In 1954, the U.S. Supreme Court announced that state-mandated segregation in public schools violated the Equal Protection Clause of the Fourteenth Amendment. Chief Justice Earl Warren wrote for a unanimous Court in *Brown v. Board of Education*: "Segregation of white and colored children in public schools has a detrimental effect upon the colored children. The impact is greater when it has the sanction of the law, for the policy of separating the races is usually interpreted as denoting the inferiority of the negro group. We conclude that, in the field of public education, the doctrine of 'separate but equal' has no place." Once again we were a nation of law, the oracles of the High Court having spoken.[11]

But in reply southern members of Congress unanimously voted the following manifesto:

The unwarranted decision of the Supreme Court in the public school cases is now bearing the fruit always produced when men substitute naked power for established law. . . . We regard the decisions of the Supreme Court in the school cases as a clear abuse of judicial power. It climaxes a trend in the Federal Judiciary undertaking to legislate, in derogation of the authority of Congress, and to encroach upon the reserved rights of the States and the people.

These members of Congress announced their intention of using all legal means possible to resist the implementation of a Supreme Court decision. In effect, they had resurrected the doctrine of nullification. Bear in mind that this was no rabble with pitchforks. These were the democratically elected members of Congress from the southern states. They were lawgivers whose view of the Constitution, they claimed, was more accurate than that of nine undemocratically chosen justices.[12]

We are and have always been a nation of laws, but whose laws, written for whom, is the question. Legal history provides an answer.

## I

## *Contested Categories*

An ironic constant of American legal culture is elected officials' "angry jibes at the complexities and burdens of the law." Determining which laws apply to which situations is a burden, even for experts in the law. The effort to make sensible arrangements of categories of law is a monumental task. The legal intellect strains to put each category into its own box, with its own rules, but the categories refuse to behave themselves. They strain to escape their confinement. Their parts carry on internecine warfare. The result is a cross-hatching pattern of laws, bold attempts to reach general principles undermined by mincing cavils of detail.[1]

The jumping bean–like quality of legal categories owes itself in part to the politics of lawmaking. Our nation of laws is also a nation of politics. Politicians in the courts, politicians in the legislatures, and politicians in executive offices make and interpret laws. But as much as one might wish to blame the problem on the politicians, the law itself is convoluted because so many different groups want law to protect or favor their interests.

The result is a law sometimes at war with itself, welcoming simultaneous opposing notions, absorbing and regurgitating contradictions, and otherwise accommodating illogical conclusions.

Whether seen from without, as a product of political demands, or from within, as a self-absorbed, self-generating process, the laws of this nation of laws can be bewildering. In fact, the most striking pattern within the categories of law is often their internal contradictions.

## *The Constitution and Constitutionalism*

When an American is opposed to something even vaguely official he or she will pronounce with vigor and certainty, "that's a violation of the Constitution." He or she may offer no evidence of a specific violation of a particular provision of the Constitution. He or she does not need to do so. The invocation of the Constitution is enough. It is as close to sacred scripture as the secular law can come.

That is so because the imposing shadow of the federal Constitution falls over all American legal history. As Chief Justice John Marshall wrote in *Marbury v. Madison* (1803): "In declaring what shall be the supreme law of the land, the Constitution itself is first mentioned; and not the laws of the United States generally, but those only which shall be made in pursuance of the Constitution, have that rank." Marshall reminded Americans of what they had achieved when they ratified the federal Constitution. "That the people have an original right to establish, for their future government, such principles as, in their opinion, shall most conduce to their own happiness, is the basis on which the whole American fabric has been erected. . . . The principles, therefore, so established are deemed fundamental. And as the authority, from which they proceed, is supreme, and can seldom act, they are designed to be permanent."[2]

Since its ratification in 1788, the federal Constitution has been America's fundamental law. Upon its broad base the framers built their governments, and to it controverted federal and state law and judicial opinions may always be referred. It was not a long document, and much in it was left for later interpretation. It was thus a living document, capable of flexible responses to new problems. But that very generality and flexibility opened the way to uncertainty and conflict. Was the Constitution a compact among sovereign states that could be undone by any of them? Did the Constitution give to the federal government the power to oversee and alter state laws? What were the relationships among the various branches of the federal government? Which of those branches had the final say in determining the meaning and application of the Constitution? Over these questions advocates of strong central government did battle with supporters of states' rights, while defenders of majoritarian rule struggled to find common ground with proponents of the rights of minorities.

The federal Constitution did not create a central government like that of France, whose departments or divisions are agencies of the central administration. Instead, Americans have both a national government and state governments. The federal Constitution's Supremacy Clause makes the national government supreme, but the state governments retain their sovereignty. This system, called federalism, was innovative when James Madison proposed it to the constitutional convention in Philadelphia. Madison recognized that the new system was an experiment, and that the concept of federalism was designed to check power rather than define it. Federalism, then, did not establish a fixed boundary between central and peripheral power, nor did it specify in explicit terms the actual relations between states and nation.

In the early years of the new nation, the new federalism did not end controversy over the powers and functions of government so much as create a new arena for it. The enumerated powers (those granted specifically to the federal government in the Constitution, such as the authority to make war, coin money, and impose tariffs) and the reserved powers (those retained by the states) were contested from the very first session of Congress. When in 1798 Vice President Thomas Jefferson, Congressman James Madison, and their Republican Party cohorts objected to the ruling Federalist Party's 1798 Alien and Sedition Acts (punishing people who criticized the Federalist administration), the two men asked state legislatures to interpose themselves between their citizens and the federal government. Interposition evolved into the doctrine of nullification when South Carolina legislators, objecting to the 1828 protective tariff, asked John C. Calhoun to expand on the interposition doctrine.

Calhoun's "Exposition" argued that a state could nullify the operation of a federal law within the state's boundaries. To support nullification, Calhoun proposed an entirely new idea of the Constitution. He called it a compact among the various states, in which any of them could negate an act of Congress. In 1832, South Carolina passed an ordinance declaring that the tariff was "null and void" in the state's ports. President Andrew Jackson's response, on December 10, 1832, was a proclamation that the Constitution "forms a government, not a league" and if South Carolina officials (or anyone else) hindered the collection of the tariff, he would use force to collect it. Clearly, constitutional law did not provide a mechanism for ending controversy between states or a state and the federal government short of the use of actual force, a fact that Abraham Lincoln found incontrovertible during the Civil War.[3]

The natural end of the strong version of state's rights was not nullification but secession. Lincoln, a very able lawyer, interpreted the Constitution to mean that the Union was indissoluble, and thus for Lincoln, as for much of his Republican Party, secession was insurrection. Lincoln never recognized the Confederacy as a sovereign government nor its laws as binding, even on the citizens of the seceding states. But no confederate southerner was executed for levying war against the nation even though the definition of treason in the federal Constitution was "levying war" against the United States. Lincoln's plan for reunion required only that one-tenth of the eligible male population of the former confederate states take an oath of allegiance to the United States and the state governments ratify the Thirteenth Amendment, ending slavery.

But federalism provided no clear mechanism for reintegrating the seceding states into the Union. The Reconstruction Era (1865–1870) saw the federal government grow in power in relation to the states, but that power was limited by the will of northern legislators to continue the integration of the freedmen and women into the legal regime—a willingness that faltered after 1876. Indeed, even the notion of nullification was not interred once and for all. State courts continued to interpret the meaning of the federal constitution to expand the power of the state at the expense of the federal government. Although the so-called Reconstruction Amendments concluded with the command that no state prohibit voting based on a man's race or color, southern states added to their constitutions grandfather clauses, literacy tests, and poll taxes that effectively barred freedmen from exercising their right to vote.

Perhaps the competing versions of federalism were inevitable. For in many ways the confederation created by the Articles of Confederation survived in the federal system. The Constitution bore the marks of a compact among sovereign states, a kind of treaty. For example, the provisions of the Full Faith and Credit Clause of Article IV are derived from the international law concept of choice of law when one nation's courts heard a dispute whose location was a second nation.

In this age of globalism the Constitution's ties to international law become even more evident. The Constitution provides for subjects central to international law, including making war and peace, treaty obligations, recognition of other nations, dealing with foreign emissaries and currencies, and tariffs. Federal courts have on occasion cited customary international law as "background rules" for deciding cases involving foreign nationals. Over the years since its ratification, the Constitution has become part of international law, serving as a model for those who wish to fabricate or revise their own constitutions. In the nineteenth century, the federal Constitution was copied by Latin American countries. In the twentieth century, newly emerging African countries borrowed from the U.S. Constitution.[4]

But insofar as a nation of laws overlaps the law of nations, America's record on international law was and remains incomplete and puzzling. The United States did not join the League of Nations after World War I, but was a prime mover of the United Nations after World War II. The United States was a signatory to the Geneva Conventions on prisoners of war but violated those conventions after 9/11. The United States supported the International Court of Justice (World Court) of the United Nations but refuses to support the International Criminal Court. Particular domestic and diplomatic events explain these zigs and zags, but another general phenomenon is apparent. The nation of laws is not always committed to an international rule of law.

## Law and Lawlessness

Americans' passion for law itself frames the second of the great themes of American legal history, matched by its opposite—Americans' willingness to take the law into their own hands. The nation was conceived in law. As if instinctively opposed to the disorder the Revolution loosed, the Continental Congress ordered the preparation of Articles of Confederation. The states ratified these in 1781. Individual states fashioned their own constitutions. The federal Constitution was an entirely new document, going into operation after nine of the thirteen states ratified it. Cities refashioned their old charters to transform themselves from independent corporations into agencies of the states, though the cities retained the power to elect their own officials and pass necessary ordinances.

So strong was the instinct of lawmaking that just about every private organization from the Boy Scouts of America and the 4H to the National Association for the Advancement of Colored People and the National Association of Manufacturers has some form of constitution or bylaws. Even the American Historical Association sought and gained a charter from the U.S. Congress in 1898 "for the promotion of historical studies, the collection and preservation of historical manuscripts, and for kindred purposes in the interest of American history and of history in America."[5]

Another proof of Americans' love of law is their attachment to litigation. The first great surge in litigation came in the 1720s, when the end of war in Europe led colonial merchants to purchase more goods than they could afford from English and Scottish merchants. Lawsuits over unpaid bills and debts flooded the colonial courts. The jump from 1710 to 1730 was more than 225 percent, and in some of the port cities one out of every ten adults was involved in some way in a lawsuit. Every period of economic downturn brought an upturn in litigation, driven by creditors trying to recover from debtors.[6]

There is some evidence that the rate of litigation, the number of people who file lawsuits divided by the number of adults in the population who can file suits, has actually declined over time. St. Louis, Missouri, civil litigation rates, for example, were far higher in the 1820s and 1830s than they are today. Today, personal bankruptcy laws, alternative dispute resolution programs, federal and state laws requiring title insurance in real estate and deposit insurance for banks, along with other institutionalized means of settling or offsetting disputes lower the rate of litigation. As well, as accidents prevalent at the inception of industrialization, for example on railroads and in mills, were reduced by one means or another, litigation over personal injuries declined. On the other hand, the volume of federal litigation has risen as new forms of entitlement, for example Social Security and Medicare benefits, were introduced and civil rights law opened federal courts to suits against racial and sexual discrimination.[7]

The modern litigation rate is a little over 200 lawsuits per 100,000 people. Tort suits (civil wrongs including everything from medical malpractice to slip and fall) accounted for about 10 percent of these. According to Rand Corporation's Institute for Civil Justice, in 1985, 911,000 tort suits were filed in federal and state courts. Most of these involved auto accidents. If tort suits are about 10 percent of the total number of suits filed (with the understanding that most suits filed do not go to trial), then the total would be about 4,000 suits per 100,000 people per year, or 4 out of every 100 people going to law per year. Omit the minors in the population, and the rate would be about 6 out of every 100 adults paying lawyers to file suits.[8]

Most litigation today arises from domestic disputes, including divorce and child custody, automobile accidents, and civil rights cases. This was not always true. In the colonial era the most common suits were for debt, defamation, and trespass on land. The economy fostered a surge in litigation in times of "bust" or recession, when businesses failed and creditors sued. Serious depressions hit the nation in the 1780s, from 1819 to 1823, from 1837 to 1843, and in 1857. After the Civil War, the depressions of 1873, 1893, and 1904 prefigured the Great Depression of 1929–1941and the serious recession that began in 2008. Bank foreclosures on unpaid mortgages, personal and business bankruptcy, and bank collapses fostered litigation. Modern personal bankruptcy laws and mortgage insurance have reduced the number of these suits, but they are still common, particularly when the mortgages are bundled into complex derivatives and the insurance for these is the unregulated "credit default swap." Surges in litigation can clog court dockets and delay the resolution of lawsuits for years on end.

At any time, the government itself can jam the courts' dockets by launching a campaign against crime. The "war on drugs" clogged the federal dockets in the 1980s, just as the prohibition campaign of the 1920s all but shut down the federal courts. By contrast, when Congress passes an act limiting the power of pensioners or medical care beneficiaries to sue their healthcare providers, the court dockets lighten. The results of such so-called reforms can be complicated and may not affect the market for litigation in the manner expected by their advocates. Caps on awards for medical malpractice designed to reduce the insurance burden on doctors, for example, did not lead to a reduction in malpractice premiums. Instead, they led many lawyers to refuse to represent victims of alleged malpractice because the cap prohibited litigating the issues fully.[9]

Lawyers are aware of trends in litigation and sometimes try to piggyback on successful suits. Mass tort suits involving asbestos, Agent Orange, intrauterine devices, tobacco use, and lead paint offered windfall damage awards to the first plaintiffs. An explosion of filings followed, and lawyers and their clients (indeed, some lawyers talked clients into suing) jumped on the bandwagon. There are more than 1,200,000 lawyers in America today, most supported by the "billable hours" of litigation or by contingency fees for successful suits. Some of these suits spill over into disputes about the size and apportioning of lawyers' fees.[10]

But the nation of laws is also a nation of the lawless. Lawlessness and extra-legal self-help in America takes many forms. It may be brazen and violent. Lynch mobs, vigilantes, and rioters of all stripes take the law into their own hands. Abolitionist William Lloyd Garrison was the first to give currency to the term "lynching" in the 1830s, recalling a self-appointed Virginia magistrate named Charles Lynch who practiced a hangman's self-help during the American Revolution. By the 1840s, lynch mobs had adopted the term as their own, proudly calling themselves "Judge Lynch's boys."[11]

Ida B. Wells, a heroic African American enemy of lynch law, in 1900 wrote that southern whites who hanged African American men "openly avow that there is an 'unwritten law' that justifies them in putting human beings to death without complaint under oath, without trial by jury, without opportunity to make defense, and without right of appeal." Wells later calculated that in 1892, 243 men and women were hanged without a trial, 160 of whom were black. The vast majority of the cases came from the Deep South. The Tuskegee Institute in Alabama was also collecting figures. Between the years 1882 and 1951, 4,730 people were lynched in the United States: 3,437 black and 1,293 white.[12]

The term "vigilante" entered the American lexicon as a shortened form of the "vigilance committee." Vigilante groups were self-appointed police forces whose activities included investigation, arrest, trial, and execution of sentence. Flourishing in the California gold fields and cities like San Francisco and Oakland after the Gold Rush of 1849, the vigilantes had no formal legal basis but exercised great power. For a time in 1856, they confronted and overcame the city, state, and federal government representatives in San Francisco. Numbering in the thousands, they disarmed the militia, imprisoned the attorney general, and claimed that they alone would deal out justice. The Committee of 1856 lasted only ninety-nine days, but its bravado (including a number of executions) demonstrated how popular the movement could become.[13]

Sometimes vigilante posses became mobs. Mobs and rioting are as old as America, and mob leaders often claimed for themselves the mantle of lawgiver. For example, the "Regulators" of North Carolina in the 1760s saw themselves as purging corrupt judges by driving them from their benches. In the spring of 1768, a band of Regulators was intercepted outside of Hillsborough, in the center of the colony, by the sheriff and other officers. What should have been a grievance session became a small riot in which some Regulators fired shots into the home of Edmund Fanning, a lawyer and clerk of the county court that sat in the town. Then they "broke and entered his mansion house, destroyed every article of furniture. . . . His papers were carried into the streets by armfuls and destroyed, his wearing apparel shared the same fate." A local farmer named Herman Husband agreed to negotiate a settlement and found himself under arrest. Seven hundred men marched into Hillsborough the next day and the authorities prudently released Husband and other prisoners to the custody of the mob.[14]

But even the lynchers, the vigilantes, and the regulators claimed that they acted only because the civilly constituted authorities were unwilling or unable to provide justice. Self-help was not the opposite of lawfulness, it was a kind of replacement, a bizarrely refracted image of law.

Not all extra-legal activity is violent. "Civil disobedience" violates law for a higher moral purpose in the eyes of the violator. The author and philosopher Henry David Thoreau went to jail rather than pay taxes that would be used to prolong the Mexican-American War and, he feared, expand the territory of slavery. In his 1849 essay "Resistance to Civil Government," he wondered

> Can there not be a government in which majorities do not virtually decide right and wrong, but conscience?—in which majorities decide only those questions to which the rule of expediency is applicable? Must the citizen ever for a moment, or in the least degree, resign his conscience to the legislator? . . . How does it become a man to behave toward this American government to-day? I answer, that

he cannot without disgrace be associated with it. I cannot
for an instant recognize that political organization as my
government which is the slave's government also.

The purpose of civil disobedience is not disorder, however, but
the reform of law. Thoreau wanted an end to the Mexican
American War, which Congress and President James K. Polk
refused to furnish. Civil disobedience in the form of nonviolent
protest became a staple of some civil rights leaders' methods.[15]

Extra-legal self-help may fashion its own law when written
law does not reach a community or the people in a community
find the strictures of the law too confining. In 1620, the Pilgrims,
arriving on the *Mayflower* at what is now Provincetown, Cape
Cod, worried that the impious among them would not comport
themselves in good order. The Pilgrims had agreed to be the
agents of the Virginia Company of Plymouth, gathering and
transshipping beaver pelts. But the charter of the company did
not provide rules for piety, so the leaders of the colony wrote a
"compact" that bound all the settlers to "covenant and combine
ourselves together into a civil Body Politick, for our better
Ordering and Preservation, and Furtherance of the Ends afore-
said; And by Virtue hereof to enact, constitute, and frame, such
just and equal Laws, Ordinances, Acts, Constitutions and Offices,
from time to time, as shall be thought most meet and convenient
for the General good of the Colony; unto which we promise all
due submission and obedience."[16]

Similarly, wagon train members going west on the Overland
Trail in the 1840s and 1850s elected leaders and framed ordinances to keep order on the journey. David Campbell recalled
that when his wagon train set out for California, in 1846, "we
organized, divided, into companies of twenty-five to thirty wagons, each company electing its own captain." The rules of each
company of wagons covered the minute detail of life on the trail.
"The company that I was in made it a rule that if they could find

a suitable place to camp they would always lay over one day in every week in order to rest up and do their washing."[17]

Community-based alternatives to federal or state law are not limited to distant times and exotic locales. In metropolitan New York City, communities of ultra-orthodox Jews called Hasidim arrange their lives around self-imposed halakhic laws of diet, dress, marriage, worship, and business relations. Courts of rabbis arbitrate disputes within the community according to these rules. On occasion, those disputes spill out into the wider world. State courts have taken the rabbinical law into account in deciding these cases. For example, in 1952, New Jersey Superior Court Judge J. S. Colie relied on orthodox Jewish law to settle a suit over the removal of a coffin from a Jewish cemetery. "This court is not bound by the ecclesiastical law. That is too well established to need citation of authorities. But it is equally well established that, while not bound by the ecclesiastical law in any given case, the court, in arriving at its decision, should consider the ecclesiastical law and give to it such weight as will bring out an equitable result."[18]

The juxtaposition of Americans' infatuation with litigation in the normal courts of law and their willingness to turn to self-help when law seems inadequate to their desires is not a measure of a weak legal system or inconsistent legal norms. Instead, both grow from the same root cause—Americans' fascination with law.

## Church and State

In the New Jersey cemetery case, the judge quoted another case of a disputed burial in a cemetery. It occurred in Brooklyn, New York, in 1926, and found its way to the highest court in the state. There, Chief Judge Benjamin Cardozo, later to be elevated to the U.S. Supreme Court, opined that

> only some rare emergency could move a court of equity to take a body from its grave in consecrated ground and put it in ground unhallowed if there was good reason to suppose that the conscience of the deceased, were he alive, would be outraged by the change. Subordinate in importance, and yet at times not wholly to be disregarded, are the sentiments and usages of the religious body which confers the right of burial.

All other considerations being equal, the state and its highest court would weigh religious sentiments in the scales of justice. "Sentiments and usages, devoutly held as sacred, may not be flouted for caprice."[19]

In a nation of laws what place does faith have? How is it permissible for courts to look to religious law and religious sentiments to decide a case when the First Amendment forbids Congress from the establishment of a religion and the Fourteenth Amendment applies this rule to the states? The struggle to find a middle ground between this stark prohibition and the pervasive religiosity of many Americans is a work in progress, still troubling to many who wonder if they should obey laws that forbid or curb faith. Although so-called faith-based initiatives like school vouchers are now the law of the land and a White House Office of Faith-Based and Neighborhood Partnerships was established in 2001and remains active, the struggle over church and state in the law goes back to the founding of the nation and will certainly continue.

Most of the American colonies had "established churches" in which only one sect was allowed to hold religious services and residents of the colony were taxed to maintain that sect. Many of the American revolutionary leaders objected to laws that favored one religious denomination over another. Rhode Island, Pennsylvania, and Virginia led the way in ending state churches.

In reply to an 1802 letter from the Baptist Association of

Danbury, Connecticut, at a time when the Baptists were among the disfavored religious sects in that state (Connecticut had established the Presbyterian Church), President Thomas Jefferson explained why religious liberty was necessary in a nation of laws.

> Believing with you that religion is a matter which lies solely between man & his god, that he owes account to none other for his faith or his worship, that the legitimate powers of government reach actions only, and not opinions, I contemplate with sovereign reverence that act of the whole American people which declared that their legislature should make no law respecting an establishment of religion, or prohibiting the free exercise thereof, thus building a wall of separation between church and state.

Jefferson referred to the language of the First Amendment to the Federal Constitution, "Congress shall make no law respecting an establishment of religion, or prohibiting the free exercise thereof." His interpretation of that law was broad—not only was Congress forbidden from favoring any particular religion over another, the government was not to meddle with freedom that men and women had to worship, or not worship, as they chose.[20]

Although no state has an established church today, the law still favors certain religious concepts over others and exempts certain religions from the operation of state laws. Sunday closing laws, for example, favor Christianity over other religions that do not regard Sunday as the Sabbath or do not have a Sabbath day. Federal tax law allows churches to register as tax-exempt bodies. In some situations, law permits public school funds use for sectarian purposes.

Even this degree of accommodation between church and state is not sufficient for some believers. Devoutly Christian lawyers and judges have never been happy with the "wall of separation" between church and state. Ever since the 1880s there have been attempts to amend the Constitution to say that Jesus Christ was the true savior and that all laws must conform to his teachings. Justice David J. Brewer, writing for the High Court in *Church of the Holy Trinity v. U.S.* (1892), announced that "the United States is a Christian Nation. . . . If we examine the constitutions of the various states, we find in them a constant recognition of religious obligations . . . and an assumption that its influence in all human affairs is essential to the well-being of the community." In lectures he gave at Haverford College thirteen years later he repeated his own opinion in *Holy Trinity* as though it was the law of the land: "This republic is classified among the Christian Nations of the world. It was so formally declared by the Supreme Court in *Church of the Holy Trinity.*"[21]

Brewer's view has not been adopted by the Court, but in *Van Orden v. Perry* (2005) a majority of the U.S. Supreme Court found that the display of the Ten Commandments was permissible on the grounds of government buildings. The monument sat at the foot of the hill atop which the Texas Statehouse stands. One could not approach the statehouse from the base of the hill, the main entrance to the grounds, without passing the monument. Chief Justice William H. Rehnquist, writing for the majority, reported that "The [federal] District Court . . . determined that a reasonable observer, mindful of the history, purpose, and context [of the display], would not conclude that this passive monument conveyed the message that the State was seeking to endorse religion. The Court of Appeals affirmed the District Court's holdings with respect to the monument's purpose and effect. We . . . now affirm" the lower courts' views.

But conceding the contradiction, the chief justice felt compelled to explain,

> Our institutions presuppose a Supreme Being, yet these institutions must not press religious observances upon

their citizens. One face looks to the past in acknowledgment of our Nation's heritage, while the other looks to the present in demanding a separation between church and state. Reconciling these two faces requires that we neither abdicate our responsibility to maintain a division between church and state nor evince a hostility to religion by disabling the government from in some ways recognizing our religious heritage.[22]

Justice John Paul Stevens and two of his fellow justices dissented. "The message transmitted by Texas' chosen display is quite plain: This State endorses the divine code of the 'Judeo-Christian' God." It was the same message that Justice Brewer had approved, but Stevens and the other dissenters believed that

> Government's obligation to avoid divisiveness and exclusion in the religious sphere is compelled by the Establishment and Free Exercise Clauses, which together erect a wall of separation between church and state. This metaphorical wall protects principles long recognized and often recited in this Court's cases. The first and most fundamental of these principles, one that a majority of this Court today affirms, is that the Establishment Clause demands religious neutrality—government may not exercise a preference for one religious faith over another.[23]

The sharply divided opinions of a sharply divided Court in *Van Orden* mirror the ambivalence within the law of church and state. That ambivalence spills out into all manner of legal matters not on their face religious. For example, the controversy over the right to an abortion is, for many, a test of religious faith. As well, the battle over gay and lesbian rights is undergirded by religious notions. Thus far, the wall of separation remains, but it is not so well mortised or so high as it had been. As Sarah Gordon has wisely written, "The place where religion and law meet has also been the place where believers' highest hopes for their country meet their darkest fears." Never the Christian Nation that believers wanted, the United States is not quite the "secular behemoth" they denounce. The politics of lawmaking had brought church and state much closer together, but the distance that remained between the civil state and the sectarian one still prevented conflict between sects and the rights of conscience for believers and nonbelievers.[24]

### Inclusion and Exclusion

In a nation of laws, who belongs and who does not? Who shall have the full bundle of liberty's blessings? Who shall toil on its soil or in its factories but every day face the danger of deportation or imprisonment? Belonging is "a basic human need," and a nation of laws cannot ignore such needs. But immigration law reflects the lack of consensus about these questions, a quandary that goes back to the revolutionary era of our laws and remains today.[25]

Belonging is the core of immigration law. Individual colonies "warned out" undesired newcomers (largely because they could not support themselves and would become a burden on the parish or the wardens of the poor), but the need for labor was so great that few overall restrictions were placed on immigrants. At the same time, colonial authorities refused to grant full rights to religious and racial minorities entering the colonies. The revolutionaries extolled the new nation as the asylum of liberty in which refugees from European tyranny might find safe haven, but two generations later, in the Alien and Enemy Alien Acts, Congress extended the naturalization period for all immigrants and gave to the president almost unlimited discretion to expel them.

For those who came, the ideal was the notion of belonging,

being a full partner in the American dream. As Barack Obama, then a law professor turned local organizer turned state politician, wrote in his *Dreams from My Father*: "Within the capital building of a big industrial state one sees every day the face of a nation in constant conversation: inner city mothers and corn and bean farmers, immigrant day laborers alongside suburban investment bankers—all jostling to be heard, all ready to tell their stories." Obama knew firsthand about immigrants—his father, whose visa had expired, had little choice but to return to his native Nigeria. Born in Hawai'i, however, Barack was as much an American citizen as anyone else.[26]

Obama belonged because Wong Kim Ark belonged. Wong was born in San Francisco to Chinese immigrants. In 1895 he returned from a visit to China and was detained at the Port of San Francisco under a law that forbade Chinese immigration. The Civil Rights Act of 1866 had defined as citizens "all persons born in the United States" but added that such individuals be not subjects of a foreign power. The Fourteenth Amendment repeated the first part of this language, "All persons born or naturalized in the United States and subject to the jurisdiction thereof, are citizens of the United States and of the State wherein they reside," but omitted the qualifier that excluded individuals subject to a foreign power.

When the detention and prospective deportation of Kim Wong Ark came to the High Court, in 1898, Justice Horace Gray wrote:

> It is beyond doubt that, before the enactment of the Civil Rights Act of 1866 or the adoption of the Constitutional Amendment, all white persons, at least, born within the sovereignty of the United States, whether children of citizens or of foreigners, excepting only children of ambassadors or public ministers of a foreign government, were native-born citizens of the United States. In the

forefront, both of the Fourteenth Amendment of the
Constitution, and of the Civil Rights Act of 1866, the
fundamental principle of citizenship by birth within the
dominion was reaffirmed in the most explicit and
comprehensive terms.

There is no mention of race, creed, color, sex, nation of origin,
class, or status in the opinion; born in America meant just that.[27]

But as much as Wong's and Obama's experience with the
law testify that the defining characteristic of citizenship is inclusion, so one can find evidence of selective exclusion in the immigration story. Some immigrants belonged less than others.

The determinant was race. The first restriction on immigration was based on African origins. The federal Constitution permitted Congress to bar the importation of slaves from overseas
in 1808. A category of people many of whom already were
denied inclusion in the polity became the first subject for exclusion from the country. This process, by which law abetted or
fomented distinctions of inclusion and exclusion based on the
notion of race and racial characteristics, would become a hallmark of immigration law.

In 1875, Congress passed the first restrictive statute for
immigration, barring convicts and prostitutes from entering the
country. The 1875 act also banned the "coolie-labor" contract
under which many Chinese were recruited to work in mines and
lay railroad track. In 1882, Congress added the Chinese Exclusion Act, prohibiting the in-migration of Chinese laborers for ten
years and presumptively forbidding courts to admit Chinese
already in the United States to citizenship. Justice Field explained
why the High Court found constitutional a provision of the act
barring Chae Chan Ping, a Chinese man who already had citizenship, from returning to the United States after a visit home.
Field explained that the Chinese

were generally industrious and frugal. Not being
accompanied by families except in rare instances, their
expenses were small and they were content with the
simplest fare, such as would not suffice for our laborers
and artisans. The competition between them and our
people was for this reason altogether in their favor, and
the consequent irritation, proportionately deep and bitter,
was followed, in many cases, by open conflicts, to the
great disturbance of the public peace. The differences of
race added greatly to the difficulties of the situation.
Notwithstanding the favorable provisions of the new
articles of the treaty of 1868, by which all the privileges,
immunities, and exemptions were extended to subjects of
China in the United States which were accorded to
citizens or subjects of the most favored nation, they
remained strangers in the land, residing apart by
themselves and adhering to the customs and usages of
their own country. It seemed impossible for them to
assimilate with our people or to make any change in their
habits or modes of living. As they grew in numbers each
year, the people of the coast saw, or believed they saw, in
the facility of immigration and in the crowded millions of
China, where population presses upon the means of
subsistence, great danger that at no distant day that
portion of our country would be overrun by them unless
prompt action was taken to restrict their immigration.

In short, the Chinese were too different, too foreign, and too
competitive to be allowed to remain. Justice Field and a majority
of his brethren did not even trust the Chinese to give truthful
evidence of their birthplace under oath.[28]

Behind the exclusionary impulse was a powerful ideology
that combined law and "blood." It was assumed by the judges

and the members of Congress that there was a sort of Anglo-Saxon or Teutonic legal spirit, a spirit of enterprise and order that was carried in the blood of these ruling races, an "ethnic superiority of Anglo-Saxons as legal actors." This almost mystical legal spirit permitted the ruling races to extend (or impose) their laws on the heathens of Africa and Asia and to exclude these same supposedly inferior peoples domiciled in the United States from the rights the ruling race had running in its blood. In this sense, *Kim Wong Ark* was the exception, not the rule. (The same justification served for American imperial ventures in the late nineteenth and early twentieth centuries.)[29]

How could law include Kim Wong Ark and exclude Chae Chan Ping? Like the white queen at breakfast in *Alice in Wonderland*, inconsistency was no problem for immigration laws. One might offer as explanation the close tie between immigration law and labor supply. Despite the rise of the new brand of nativist legalism in the 1880s and 1890s, immigration of non–Anglo Saxon peoples to the United States virtually exploded. Expanding needs in industrial labor, mining, and railroad construction welcomed cheap labor, and that is what the immigrants offered. Between 1880 and 1920, almost 24 million immigrants arrived in the United States. These immigrants were primarily from southern and eastern European countries. In 1882, immigration reached a new high with 788,992 persons arriving that year. By 1920 nearly 14 million out of the 105 million people living in the United States were foreigners. In 1920–1921, approximately 800,000 people came to the United States; about two-thirds of that number were from southern and eastern Europe. They had fled from a Europe torn by war and impoverishment to the American shore, passing in the harbor of New York City a statue of liberty. In 1912, at its base was carved: "From her beacon-hand / Glows world-wide welcome; her mild eyes command / The air-bridged harbor that twin cities frame. / 'Keep ancient lands, your storied pomp!' cries she / With silent lips. 'Give me your tired, your poor, / Your huddled masses yearning to breathe free, / The wretched refuse of your teeming shore. / Send these, the homeless, tempest-tost to me, / I lift my lamp beside the golden door!'"[30]

But the depression of 1903 curtailed that demand, and nativism gained new influence in the law. In 1917, Congress added a literacy test for immigrants. In 1921, with the demand for labor declining further, Congress enacted the Emergency Quota Act, the first explicitly quantitative immigration law. In any given year, immigrants of any nationality could not exceed 3 percent of the number of that nationality living in the United States according to the 1910 census. The Immigration Act of 1924 made the quota system permanent and reduced the percentage of immigrants of any nationality allowed into the United States to 2 percent based on the 1890 census. In 1890, the great influx from the south of Europe had not yet begun. Thus the supposedly racially inferior southern European, the Italian and the Jew from the Pale, were effectively barred from the United States.

A more recent spate of immigration laws is just as at war with itself as earlier immigration regulations. In 1986, Congress passed the Immigration Reform and Control Act. The act provided for summary process to expel suspected illegal immigrants, a category that not surprisingly turned out to be composed of Latinos and Asians. In 1996, the Antiterrorism and Effective Death Penalty Act passed into law, expanding the grounds of deportation for immigrants convicted of crimes. The Personal Responsibility and Work Opportunity Reconciliation Act of 1996 made permanent resident aliens ineligible for most federal benefits. The Illegal Immigrant Responsibility Act of 1996 expedited deportation, made entry into the country harder, and imposed time limitations for filing asylum claims.[31]

From the inception of the nation, the law of belonging warred with itself. Labor scarcity beckoned those beyond our gates to come and work; competition for scarce jobs closed the doors of immigration. It seemed that the law followed obediently behind the economics of labor scarcity and surplus. But not always. For racism might close doors on newcomers and idealism might still open them.

## Democracy or Expertise?

The glory of American governance is its democratic character. More officers, legislators, judges, and executives are elected in this country than any other, and the franchise, despite its initial limitations, was broader in the United States than (until the post–World War II years) any other country. Democracy gave a certain populist tone, for want of a better word, to American law. The gift of millions of acres of federal land to homesteaders during and after the Civil War was an act of populist lawmaking. Populist Party platforms in the 1880s and 1890s, including certain kinds of nationalization of industries, have become part of the legal regime. Although the narrowly rural objectives of the Populist Party may not have survived (save in concerts for "Farm Aid") the ideals of racial unity and greater class equality are alive and well.[32]

Such democracy may have an ugly underside. Majorities, the lever arm of democracies, may wear the face of bigotry. Manipulated by a skillful opinion leader with less-than-honorable purposes in mind, the mob may cast itself as the majority and scourge the land of infidelity, immorality, or any form of deviance. It is especially easy for a demagogue to appeal to a majority in a democratic system under stress, for example during an economic depression or in wartime. The anti-Masonic campaigns of the 1820s and 1830s had a populist color. Campaigns against abolitionism in the 1830s and 1840s, against Catholics in the 1840s and 1850s, against the Chinese in the 1880s and 1890s, against German Americans during World War I, against Jews in the years before World War II, against suspected radicals in the 1950s, and against gays in the 1980s and 1990s had a broad democratic base. Often these movements enabled minor political parties to garner mass support.[33]

But the framers of the Constitution were not democrats and feared all the horrors, real and imagined, of democracy in practice. Their answer was more law, a "rule of law" that limited what the majority could do, finding in law "the obvious mechanism to fill the vacuum" that the absence of other means to resolve disputes and distribute value left. While the courts still fulfill that function, over the course of American legal history they have been joined by an arm of government not mentioned in the Constitution and whose mechanisms are not majoritarian at all. These are the administrative agencies. "Assignment of discretionary authority to administrative officers is one form of benefit, often serving the interests both of the government officer and of nongovernmental parties."[34]

The explosion of administrative agencies, from a handful of commissions on pensions, Indian affairs, and railroads in the nineteenth century, to the veritable alphabet soup of agencies in the Progressive and New Deal eras, was necessitated by the demands of industry, unions, and consumers. Economic democracy—a congeries of interest groups competing for the ear of government—required administrative agencies' proliferation. But the foundations of administrative law do not lie in democracy's rough and tumble. Administrative law rests upon the presumption of expertise. And expertise is elitist, not democratic. As a Brookings Institute report in 1927 concluded, "Administrative agencies can act on their own initiative, assume responsibility for determining facts, and have expert staffs to do the work of investigating. They are not bound by formal rules of evidence and procedure as are the courts, and they generally can, and do, act in a more direct, efficient, and economical manner and with much greater dispatch." After service as director of the Securities and Exchange Commission, administrative law proponent James M. Landis added that "expertise only springs from that continuity of interest, that ability and desire, to devote fifty-two weeks a year, year after year, to a particular problem." The gain was efficiency, the scientific settlement of complex problems of the economy by expert managers. The ideal was "self-executing" rules without the inconsistency or disorder of the democratic system, a machine that warred with "our humanity" and our common sense.[35]

Democratic lawmaking and administrative adjudication are in constant contention, but the opposition is not always polar. Administrative agencies are created by Congress, and Congress advises and consents on presidential nominees for seats on the agencies. They are independent but after a 1946 act of Congress, parties may appeal from the agency determinations to the federal courts. Thus democracy and expertise are in a constant state of contiguity, jostling up against one another with varying results.

The great themes of American legal history all evidence a dramatic tension—pulling in different directions, then coming together, containing within themselves contradictory impulses that cannot be contained, but are. This push and pull makes difficult any scholarly attempt to chart the trajectory of American law but does not deter us from tracking the path of the law, as we see in the next chapter.

## 2

## *Divergent Paths*

In an 1896 talk at Harvard Law School entitled "The Path of the Law," Oliver Wendell Holmes Jr. told his audience, "I wish, if I can, to lay down some first principles for the study of this body of dogma or systematized prediction which we call the law, for men who want to use it as the instrument of their business to enable them to prophesy in their turn, and, as bearing upon the study, I wish to point out an ideal which as yet our law has not attained." That ideal was "logic"—convergent, cogent, rational, unifying logic to the law. Instead, what he saw was a law whose only logic was its history.[1]

In a nation of laws like ours, were the law some expression of logic the course of its many phases and expressions would converge; surface ambivalence and contradiction would resolve themselves and reveal beneath their surface a single wholly integrated structure. One would see that the law was evolving toward a goal of uniformity and harmony. Individual observers of this process might disagree about that goal—the advancement of human dignity; the protection of private property; some utopia in which people gave according to their abilities and took according to their needs—but the goal would be attainable.

This is not what one sees when one sets the nation of laws

in historical motion. Not at all. Instead, one sees a competition among rival interests and ideas. True—the law evolved over time. New species of law appeared and old species became extinct. But the many paths of the law have not converged on consensus or harmony. Instead, a growing diversity of law seems to be the rule, some variant of the evolution of biological species. In fact, the idea of biological evolution is one guide to follow the path of American legal history.

## The Evolving Nation of Laws

To be sure, the idea of evolution is itself contested, though not by scientists. On the 200th anniversary of his birth, commentators agreed that "Darwin's theory of evolution has become the bedrock of modern biology. . . . It is a testament to Darwin's extraordinary insight that it took almost a century for biologists to understand the essential correctness of his views." Historical judgment was scarcely less enthusiastic. "The theory of evolution is arguably the greatest idea the human mind ever had."[2]

But biological scientists disagree on the mechanism of that selection. Three major variants of evolutionary theory offer alternative models for plotting the course of American law. The classical Darwinian model (Darwin's own) would posit a struggle of the fittest legal ideas and institutions to survive, "a struggle for existence leading to the preservation of profitable deviations of structure or instinct." The Darwinian model is gradual and sweeping, covering the many categories of law existing at any given time, looking for the overall pattern of their development. It is a story of competing doctrines and practices coexisting in time, jostling one another for dominant place, the loser dying off, the winner surviving to reproduce itself.[3]

A second evolutionary model of the law takes its inspiration from Stephen J. Gould's idea of "punctuated equilibria." In this theory, "A new species can arise when a small segment of the ancestral population is isolated at the periphery of the ancestral range. . . . Favorable variations spread quickly. Small peripheral isolates are a laboratory of evolutionary change." Applied to legal history, punctuated equilibrium would argue that key legal innovations take place in a small area of the law and then spread to other areas of law. The diffusion may happen virtually overnight, as a new category of law is born and flourishes safe from the competition of its older, less fit but more populous rivals.[4]

A third pattern of evolution resembles that in Richard Dawkins's *The Selfish Gene*. Richard Dawkins has proposed that it is not a competition among species for survival that determines who gets to reproduce, but a competition among individual genes. It is the genes themselves that vie to reproduce themselves, rather than the entire organism. Genes may even shorten the life of the individual animal, insect, or plant in order to insure the perpetuation of the gene pool. "I preferred to think of the gene as the fundamental unit of natural selection, and therefore the fundamental unit of self-interest," for it was the gene that had far more copies of itself than the individual plant or animal, and much more than the species.

The societal counterpart to the gene is the "meme," the social and psychological appeal of an idea, not its purely biological adaptivity. Memes compete with one another for space in our heads, just as legal ideas compete for space in the texts of the law—legislation, judicial opinions, legal scholarship. The key to a meme winning out over other memes is the way in which that meme can fit into an existing set of supportive memes. Thus legal doctrines that fit other current doctrine—for example, ideas of morality or the marketplace or politics—would be better able to survive than doctrines that ran athwart of accepted notions in other areas of intellectual endeavor.[5]

Of course, the biological analogy is only that, a way to conceptualize change in the law as a form of adaptation to its environment, in this case the changing pattern of demands on the legal system. But deployment of the evolutionary paradigm—the notion of species of law competing for available niches in the political, social, and economic surroundings—enables us to make sense of an otherwise booming, buzzing confusion of laws and legal actors. More, the analogy reveals how the contentions in the law led not to paralysis or chaos but to innovative and progressive reforms. In short, the law adapted.

### Darwinian Competition

In Charles Darwin's biological schema, evolution entailed gradual changes in the form of species over long periods of time. Darwin proposed that the species living in his day were evolved from much earlier species through a process of chance mutation and fortuitous adaptation. Similar ideas about the evolution of law were already abroad in England. Students of law like William Blackstone recognized that the legal regime in which they lived was a product of past times: "whence it is in our law the goodness of a custom depends upon its having been used time out of mind. . . . This is what gives it its weight and authority: and of this nature are the maxims and customs which compose the common law." Judges were the "living oracles" of the law, but law was not made by judges, it was discovered, so that the mainsprings of change in the law were not imposed by men, but grew out of the principles of the law itself.[6]

Other commentators on the law saw the direction and shape of its change as part of a different kind of dialectic. Positive law—the command of the state—was only a superstructure, the visible architecture of a far more foundational process. Ambiguities and contradictions in law were illusions, temporary disturbances on the surface of powerful currents of economic forces that determined the course of history. The tie between law and this kind of determinism was close. For example, the material demands of southern slavery dictated the shape of the law of slavery, and variations in that law did not cause changes in the underlying fundamental economic relationships. Thus a late antebellum movement to protect slaves from violent masters did not herald the end of the "peculiar institution," but only signaled a "paternalism" designed to make slavery appear more gentle.[7]

With or without the assumption of a deterministic mechanism for change, there is much evidence for a Darwin-like evolution of American law. After all, in many ways the law in the United States remains as it began—a federation of republican states committed to certain legal ideals, refining and reforming old common law concepts, clinging still to basic processes like trial by jury, stare decisis (following precedent), and the rule of recognition (that statutes should be interpreted in the light of constitutional provisions). The very notion of precedent (when courts look to previous decisions to decide new cases) slowed and channeled change in an evolutionary path. While the substance of legislation may change, those changes have come incrementally. "None of the changes . . . were sudden, none were quick, overnight shocks." Overall, in the evolutionary model the law that adapts itself to changes in society is the law that reproduces itself in the next generation. "American law, from its late eighteenth-century beginnings, has been self-consciously and self-critically aware of itself as a system that is supposed to make some kind of overall sense. It has never been allowed to grow in the chaotic, disorganized, unplanned" manner of other systems of law. Instead, it evolved in a rational fashion.[8]

The Darwinian model of the evolution of the law seems to fit the story of economic regulation. For the nation of laws was also the home of free markets. The changing relationship of market activity and law, that is, legal regulation of the market, demonstrates how some legal ideas defeated others as conflict between those who wish to be free of regulation and those who wish to impose it played out in legal arenas.

The interrelation of market demands and regulatory impulses was a feature of early modern English law that imperial authorities exported to the American colonies. As commerce became more important in the early modern English economy, parliament and the judges made the law friendlier to the practices of merchants. In contractual relations, older conceptions like fair exchange (that a contract should be fair to all parties) gave way to newer ideas such as bargained-for exchange (in which the parties get what they asked for, even if the transaction was unfair to one party).

At the same time, parliament passed statutes fixing prices, wages, the terms of apprenticeship, and the conduct of merchant guilds. These regulations crossed the Atlantic in the form of price and wage regulations. Some colonies even passed sumptuary laws, limiting the types of clothing the lower classes could wear. But the most important regulations in America concerned its trade with the home country. In the 1650s the English parliament began to frame a system of laws to ensure that the home country had a favorable balance of trade with all the parts of the English empire. The name of the first of the acts, later given to the whole of them (nearly 200 enactments by 1774), was the Navigation Acts, and the overarching system was mercantilism. The customs service, the royal courts, the imperial officialdom in America all had the primary purpose of ensuring that English merchants, consumers, bankers, and shippers benefited from the empire. A regulatory scheme reached deep into the colonies, surveying trees, placating Indians, setting prices and wages, denying to the colonies the right to print money policed mercantilism.

Americans chafed at these restrictions and found ways around them. There was no way to hold servants to their labor when there was no way to stop them from running away from their masters. Labor was prized and there was always a shortage of laborers. Thousands of new immigrants from Germany, Scotland, and Africa poured into the colonies each year, but the demand for labor never slackened. Imperial law forbade the printing of colonial currency (or colonial buyers of British goods would pay their debts in depreciated paper money). To get around the shortage of circulating currency and the customs duties, colonists used land bank notes and tobacco inspection certificates instead of money, traded outside of the empire with the French, the Dutch, and the Spanish, bribed customs officials to look the other way when ships bearing contraband entered harbor, and when all else failed, declared independence.

It was a near perfect example of systematic, willful, and very profitable disregard of law. How was that possible in a nation of laws—particularly when the colonists took every opportunity to say that England's laws were the best in the world, and that English law came to the colonies? Did the two halves of the colonial legal mind simply ignore one another? Was it a version of wink-wink, nod-nod, in which certain kinds of illegality were simply ignored? Not at all. It was an example of more adaptive legal forms outdueling less adaptive forms. The customs officials and other agents of the crown in the New World knew what was happening, and some complained to the home authorities. Other officials accepted the bribes and remained quiet. In any case, the precedent was set for the almost casual violation of regulatory statutes because the latter restricted the economic growth of the colonies.

Parenthetically, that widespread willingness to evade or ignore the law says something very important about Americans. When upset or affronted by some activity, pet excrement left by the curb for example, Americans demand a law. Pooper-scooper laws are now as common as leash laws in many communities. But there are some pet walkers who never scoop up their animals' droppings. They know the law and ignore it. So do violators of the posted speed limits, hunters and fishermen out of season, just about everyone who files a tax return and fudges business expenses, and litterers. Why in a nation of so many laws are there so many lawbreakers? The answer may lie in the fact that law breaking was, in some cases, adaptive behavior. Commercial survival depended on evading the customs laws. The thin line between profit and loss may depend upon a liberal view of tax exemptions. Getting somewhere a little sooner may make obeying the speed limit a burden. (Not picking up pet poop is inexcusable.) Like lawmaking and obedience to law, bending the law fit the Darwinian model best. Certainly there is even more evidence for this in the struggle between a free market and regulation of markets.

But that competition continued, as even in the heyday of free market, nineteenth-century capitalism, laws limited what railroads, innkeepers, and freight haulers could charge. The law of common carriers inherited from England prescribed the duties of freight haulers and passenger trains to their ticket holders. Regulations surrounded what kind of fence one could (or must) erect around one's property. If one farmer had a proper fence and his neighbor's pigs ate his garden crops, he had grounds for suit. In the 1830s South Carolina planters and farmers in the state assembly debated what constituted a fence, and the legislature finally conceded that a ditch of a certain width was a fence, regulating who could hunt, fish, and traverse the land bordered by the ditch.

During and after the Civil War, the federal government joined in the regulatory movement. During the war, the federal sanitary commission pioneered in regulation of hospitals, the adjutant general's commissions inspected army rations and munitions, and a new Bureau of Internal Revenue managed collection of a wide variety of new taxes. After the war, new agencies, including the Interstate Commerce Commission, provided rules for fair pricing and good practices. In the Progressive Era (1900–1920), these government agencies began to multiply. The

Food and Drug Administration and the Federal Trade Commission had investigative powers as well as advisory roles. The New Deal (1933–1941) added its quota of regulatory bodies, including the Securities and Exchange Commission, to watchdog Wall Street; the National Recovery Administration, to set and police standards for business; and the National Labor Relations Board, to provide an administrative alternative to labor-capital warfare. The number of federal and state regulatory agencies has increased since the New Deal, with new cabinet-level departments regulating transportation, energy, education, and homeland security leading the way.

From the 1870s through the 1920s, federal courts upheld the regulatory operations of the state and federal agencies when the public health and welfare was clearly at stake. When an industry, for example grain storage companies, carried on business that had a major effect on the public interest, states could regulate the prices the companies charged (*Munn v. Illinois* [1877]). In a few cases, however, the federal courts found unconstitutional a state's impositions on the conduct of business, for example a state statute limiting the hours that a bakery owner could require workers to labor (*Lochner v. New York* [1905]). Supreme Court supervision of state regulatory activity was based on a particular reading of the Fourteenth Amendment's Due Process Clause by which the Court arrogated to itself substantive review of regulations to insure that they did not impose on the constitutional rights of individuals. This posture shifted during the New Deal, when the High Court majority began to defer to state and federal regulatory statutes.

But a Darwinian contest continued within the evolving structure of administrative agencies. Regulatory agencies were captured by the very business interests they were supposed to supervise. Powerful industries exerted great influence on sitting members of an agency. It was not uncommon for outgoing agency commissioners to be offered high-level employment in the industry the agency oversaw. On occasion, new members of an agency found themselves lobbied by former commissioners. These connections undermined the original purpose of the agency, neutral and fair regulation of business practices but allowed business interests to prosper.

In the struggle between labor and capital, the Darwinian model of legal change was so obvious that late nineteenth-century contemporaries actually applied Darwinian language to it. Early in the nineteenth century, craftsmen and laborers formed associations and unions to control the conditions of their labor. State courts regarded these first labor unions as illegal conspiracies in restraint of trade, but by the end of the nineteenth century the courts conceded the legality of union organizations.

In the later portion of the century, however, business interests, aided by friendly federal courts, gained injunctions against strikes and other union activities. Congress remedied abuses of this legal power in the Clayton Antitrust Act of 1914, exempting unions from antitrust injunctions. When business-friendly courts enjoined secondary boycotts and sympathy strikes, the New Deal's Wagner National Labor Relations Act of 1935 ended these injunctions. But powerful unions and great corporations continued to compete for control of the legal apparatus governing the workplace.[9]

A resurgent Republican Congress after World War II nibbled at the edges of New Deal labor legislation. The Taft-Hartley Act of 1947 defined a series of "unfair labor practices" that unions were not to undertake, and Taft-Hartley, along with prosecutions of suspected Communists and racketeers in organized labor, led to a steep decline in labor union membership. The survival of organized labor was never assured by the law. The unions had to fight for their members' rights, a Darwinian struggle that continues to this day.

Decried by opponents as the producer of endless red tape, regulation is a fixture of the modern legal landscape. It is impossible to imagine modern life without commissions like the Environmental Protection Agency, the Occupational Safety and Health Administration, and the Federal Aviation Administration. But critics of regulation wish freer markets. As law professor Richard Epstein has written, "The champions of further regulation argue that their efforts will not limit innovations. . . . But there are no free fixes. Too often ill-designed regulation gives us the worst of both worlds—slower innovation and more limited" developmental incentive. "We have much to fear in any new round of regulation." But that new round will certainly come.[10]

Reduced to the microscopic level, the market vs. regulation struggle for survival reveals many smaller contests, cross-currents and contradictions in each stage and in the transitions from stage to stage. Within each category of law, within each jurisdiction, these competitions reproduced the struggle for survival of legal forms one can envision in the larger system, a kind of fractal-like copying and recopying of the same pattern on a smaller and smaller scale.[11]

For example, the vast extent of relatively cheap land in the West led buyers and sellers to make land sales easier than they were under English law. One had only to purchase the land, obtain a deed, and record it in the county courthouse. Disputes over land ownership were also simplified. Private land sales in the early nineteenth century required only a contract between buyer and seller. Land speculation became a national mania. Founding fathers like Benjamin Franklin and George Washington set up companies to benefit from the speculation in western land, and arch political enemies like Aaron Burr and Alexander Hamilton put aside their differences to invest in the same land schemes. The new land law was adaptive to the conditions of the new nation and so replaced older forms of land ownership, buying, and selling.

But rampant and unregulated land speculation led to violent confrontations between different groups of would-be settlers in

Pennsylvania, the Ohio country, and Georgia. The confederation government (1781–1788) responded by creating a "national domain." The government took title to all the western territories and began to regulate the survey, sale, and even the cost of every acre. Land in the national domain was sold at public auctions. What had been a relative free-for-all was, at least in theory, to become a regulated process of settlement and development. But none of these measures entirely curbed speculation or prevented violence on the frontier over competing forms of land use. Battles over free ranging cattle and hogs (farmers wanted livestock fences, ranchers wanted unregulated grazing of their stock) became the stuff of legend. The Lincoln County, New Mexico, land wars of the 1870s and 1880s, for example, gave rise to the fabled story of Billy the Kid, a hired gun during the contention between townsfolk and ranchers.

In the early republic business interests and agriculturalists battled in courts over access to flowing water—the power source for mills and factories. Farmers wanted undiminished water supplies for their crops and livestock. Millers and factory owners wanted the water channeled into mill "races" to power their machinery. The weapons of the battle were competing versions of "riparian" or water use doctrine. The manufacturers won, courts agreeing that the mills and factories were the best use of the water resources. This "instrumentalism" was the work of litigants, their lawyers and judges adopting the role of miniature legislatures to change the law to benefit one class of clients. Such shifts were adaptive in their time, but modern environmental law has once again shifted the balance in these cases, putting the industrial land user on the defensive, and protecting the quality of air, water, and land for ordinary consumers. Again, the regulation was adaptive, for the environment could not longer support unrestrained pollution. In the process, "Law is no longer merely an agency for resolving disputes; it is an active, dynamic means of social control and change."[12]

In the 1840s and 1850s, the same struggle for survival of rival legal concepts played out in eminent domain cases. In these, a government agency takes land from an owner for public use. The owner is compensated, but loses right to the property. In the nineteenth century, courts upheld eminent domain takings, deciding that the new user, most often a canal company, a railroad, or a turnpike, would put the property to better use. That approach no longer dominates eminent domain, however. In the closing years of the twentieth century and the opening of the next decade, courts have protected the property owner against local and state eminent domain takings for beach erosion, river edge conservation, and other public purposes.

Consider the law of incorporation. In the new nation, corporate charters were quasi-monopolies granted to a single company by the legislature. They were supposed to have a public purpose. So many partnerships longed to become corporations, however, that by the 1870s legislatures agreed these charters could be had by paying a licensing fee. One legal regime had succeeded another by adapting to demands in the economic environment.

The changing law of corporations encouraged businesses to incorporate in order to stimulate competition, as though unaware of the dangers of concentration of wealth. Courts protected the corporation with the legal fiction that it was a person with all the rights of a person under the Fourteenth Amendment. They also loosened the bonds holding corporate activities confined within the state that issued the charter. Charters themselves grew bloated and formless—the corporations could do pretty much what they wanted to do. They began to hold stock in one another, the largest of them becoming "trusts," giant holding companies. Other corporations colluded with one another to fix prices and control markets. By the end of the nineteenth century, consolidation, nationwide networks, quasi-monopolies, and concentration of ownership, production, and distribution within a few companies were characteristic of more than two-thirds of the economy's industrial and financial wealth. Mass markets, particularly in the cities, fostered these developments. Some states, notably Delaware and New Jersey, welcomed the corporations, giving corporations greater freedom to do as they pleased (including veiling their misconduct).

But unrestrained bigness was not adaptive and a countervailing movement was already under way. At first, legislative efforts to rein in corporations, in particular the Sherman Antitrust Act of 1890, relied on already out-of-date theories of the morality of competition among small firms in genuinely free markets. More effective legislative controls on corporate pyramiding and quasi-monopolies accepted bigness and reined in its abuses. President Theodore Roosevelt's "new nationalism" combined regulatory commissions with trust busting. The trust busters won significant victories against the most blatant abusers of corporation law such as the American Tobacco Company Trust and Standard Oil. Other huge combines, including U.S. Steel, found ways to avoid dissolution. Trust busting waxed and waned as Republican administrations favored business interests and Democratic presidents tried to reduce the power of the corporate giants. During the New Deal and World War II, government lawyers accepted the inevitability of great corporations, but negotiated an ongoing partnership between government and corporations to protect the public interest. This was necessary during the war to convert peacetime to wartime production. By contrast, organized labor's gains during the New Deal were curtailed during the war. During the 1950s, the federal government again stepped back from close scrutiny of the corporate giants, and mergers again dominated corporate life (and corporate law practice). Notable antitrust suits in recent times, for example that against the software giant Microsoft, have not prevented it from attempting to swallow smaller competitors. The struggle continues.[13]

While not so obviously a "red in tooth and claw" competition for dominance as in trust busting, a struggle for women's rights marked a Darwinian evolution of domestic relations law. Colonial law made the husband or father the legal head of the household, a miniature king in his domain. Servants were part of this household, and domestic servants were included in family law. In the early republic, servants could no longer be held to labor (domestic servants, for example, became hired maids), but children's fate still lay with their father's will, women could only with great difficulty obtain a divorce, and then custody of the children would still go to the father. With a few exceptions, a married woman had no property of her own except her personal belongings. The rest was her husband's.

Bit by bit, this scheme unraveled. In fact, the old norms of law that "the marriage relationship be kept 'sacred and inviolate' . . . had always been played out on the terrain of separation and separate identities." Increasingly, in court, women and men found ways to use the law against itself, in effect to recognize when the marriage no longer worked. By the end of the nineteenth century, women gained court-ordered divorces based on adultery, desertion, and cruelty. So, too, by state legislative action, married women could own, buy, and sell property separate from their husbands'. Aided by Victorian ideas of the purity of motherhood, courts began to give fit mothers custody of children over the claims of unfit fathers (though the fathers had to provide child support). With the amendment of the federal Constitution barring states from denying the right to vote to women came greater women's participation in the public arena.

But Victorian values and progressive reforms cut two ways. Once commonly distributed birth control information was categorized as pornography and banned from the mails. The law seemed to free women and then find new bonds for them. In the twentieth century, concepts like no-fault divorce and children's rights became the norm. As a result, the number of custody suits grew rapidly, and the wide variety of state laws and precedents on custody taxed the ingenuity of lawyers and the patience of judges. A new legal feminism seemed to have won the day in the Civil Rights Act of 1964's protections for women's equality in the workplace and education, but the apparent triumph contained a paradox. In some areas of law, women could and did claim special protections reviving in new forms the older paternalistic "protections" of a weaker sex. The battle for full legal equality is not over.[14]

A final example of Darwinian evolution of law is the law of patent and copyright. In early modern English law, the government imposed a strict regulation of print. Publications were censored and even after official censorship was lifted, there was no real freedom of the press. In the new United States, state and federal law promoted freedom of the press, with the result that editors and publishers felt free to reprint others' work without permission or payment. This new freedom was not entirely adaptive, however, for in the free market, only a property interest in one's writing rewarded authors. The same was true of invention. A love and aptitude for invention runs all through American history. New technologies in machinery, electronics, and medicine have made the United States one of the most advanced of Western nations.

The law of copyright and patent followed these countervailing interests, as back and forth they contested for access to the rewards of invention and artistry. Each new invention not only generated patent struggles, beginning with Eli Whitney's attempt to patent his cotton gin, but rival conceptions of patent law. At first, copyright and patent protection, reserved to Congress by the Constitution, was a haphazard matter. After 1793, an act of Congress mandated that patents for "meritorious" inventors were to be registered. An 1836 statute added the requirement that application was to be examined for originality. But courts refused to prevent competitors of the original patentee from developing improved versions of inventions, leading to a bewildering variety

of patents and products. The democratic instincts of the nineteenth century were nowhere more evident than in the patents
issued to inventors from all walks of life. The result was more
patents for more people than in any other nation and more litigation on patent infringement claims than in any other nation.

The federal Constitution gave to Congress exclusive authority to pass copyright laws. Congress enacted the first American
copyright law in 1790, with a revised act following in 1831 (permitting copyright of music) and further amendments in 1870,
1909, 1976, and 1998. These laws have proved hard to enforce.
Knockoff copies of novels and poems reappeared in cheap editions throughout the nineteenth century. Antebellum magazine
editors routinely reprinted other magazines' articles and essays
without permission.

After the Civil War, the number of copyrights and patents
registered grew rapidly. Popular authors like Edgar Rice Bur-
roughs pressed for extension of copyrights beyond the author's
lifetime, and giants like Thomas Alva Edison's General Electric
and George Westinghouse's laboratories staged expensive legal
battles over patent rights to electronics. Copyright and patent law
began to overlap one another as the patent and copyright holders
of new modes of electronic storage and performance machines
and the songs and books they contained did battle with those
who demanded free access to music and movies. Telegraph and
railroad patent litigation has been succeeded by software patent
litigation, and copyright disputes over song lyrics have morphed
into suits over electronic reproduction of music for personal use.
Judges issued contradictory rulings about who had copyright to
letters deposited in archives and how much of a copyrighted
book, poem, visual, or piece of music might be reproduced without gaining permission of the copyright holder, as competing
theories of fair use and property rights battled in the courts.

Over time, some legal ideas and practices came to dominate
over older forms. Competition for the available niches in the

legal order was fierce, and only the most adaptive survived. Within this overall evolution, legal combatants had arrayed themselves on different sides of issues, armed themselves with treatises and case law, and did battle over doctrine and theory. A Darwinian nation of laws was not a peaceful kingdom.

## Punctuated Equilibria

One may also conceive of evolution not as Charles Darwin did, as a gradual process based on chance mutations and adaptivity in large populations over a long period of time, but instead as a series of lurches and spurts occurring in out-of-the-way places among very small populations. In some ways, this idea of a punctuated equilibrium fits the multiple paths American law has trod far better than the Darwinian idea of gradual, general struggle for survival. In this model, a single judicial opinion or legislative act, a particularly novel notion of law published ahead of its time, a lawsuit beginning in obscurity and involving ordinary people, can re-form into a new line of doctrine, lead to new visions of rights, or otherwise profoundly alter the legal landscape.

The changes the American Revolution wrought in the law are an example of a punctuated equilibrium. John Adams thought that the Revolution only confirmed long-standing, slowly evolving concepts of rights and self-government in the colonies. The Revolution, he wrote, occurred in the hearts and minds of the people long before the war for Independence began. Traces of republican self-government in the colonies, for example in the fairly widespread right to vote among free men in most of the colonies, antedated the crisis of 1763–1776. Elements of the Bill of Rights, for example the guarantee of jury trial and access to counsel, appeared in some colonies' laws as early as the end of the seventeenth century.[15]

But the sudden burst of constitution writing following the

Declaration of Independence led to a very different legal framework than that existing before 1776. Independent republics in a confederation were not the same as colonies in an empire, and written bills of rights were not the same as customary privileges. In this sense, the leap to written constitutions limiting the powers of government was an example of punctuated equilibrium rather than evolution, a "contagion of liberty" in the words of historian Bernard Bailyn not wholly, indeed not even partly anticipated or understood by those whose words inadvertently began the process. The ambiguities still existed, but change had come in a sudden spurt instead of a steady evolution. "Thinkers at each stage, impelled by a spirit at once quizzically pragmatic and loftily idealistic, built upon the conclusions of their predecessors, and grasped implications only vaguely sensed before." The claim of rights against a corrupt imperial rule based on older Whig notions of constitutionalism transformed into the argument for bills of rights, the end of slavery, and the disestablishment of religion. And it all happened in the space of a few years.[16]

Though nothing would seem farther in time or in subject matter from the revolutionary generation's recasting of fundamental law than a lawsuit over a defective automobile tire in the early twentieth century, the two events are both examples of punctuated legal equilibria. The impact of punctuated equilibria need not be immediate. That is what "punctuated" means. The early twentieth-century rule in cases of defective products was that the buyer of a product injured by its malfunction could sue the person or the firm from which he purchased the product. To win, he needed to show "privity," or "privity of contract," the close connection between buyer and seller based on a contract or other agreement, and that the seller was liable for the defect in the product. In *MacPherson v. Buick Motor Company* (1916), Justice Benjamin Cardozo of the New York State Court of Appeals combined pieces of old law to create an entirely new doctrine of products liability.

In *MacPherson*, the buyer bought a Buick from a dealer, who got it from the manufacturer, who bought the wheels from another company. Could the buyer sue the manufacturer when the wheels literally came off? "One of the wheels was made of defective wood, and its spokes crumbled into fragments. The wheel was not made by the defendant; it was bought from another manufacturer. There is evidence, however, that its defects could have been discovered by reasonable inspection, and that inspection was omitted." The manufacturer was not trying to defraud anyone, but was negligent. Was Buick then liable for the damages?

Cardozo looked further. In cases where the product was inherently dangerous to the purchasers, a firearm, for example, or a boiler, the law already imposed on a manufacturer a special duty to insure safety. Hence the manufacturer was liable when the product failed. "If the nature of a thing is such that it is reasonably certain to place life and limb in peril when negligently made, it is then a thing of danger." Cardozo proposed that a car was such a product—a novel idea. The question then became how far back in the process of making the car and selling the car liability for a defect went. "Precedents drawn from the days of travel by stage coach do not fit the conditions of travel to-day. . . . They are whatever the needs of life in a developing civilization require them to be." By the early twentieth century, large manufacturers often assembled parts built elsewhere. The duty to inspect, and hence the liability for defects, lay with the manufacturer. "We think the defendant [Buick] was not absolved from a duty of inspection because it bought the wheels from a reputable manufacturer. It was not merely a dealer in automobiles. It was a manufacturer of automobiles. It was responsible for the finished product. It was not at liberty to put the finished product on the market without subjecting the component parts to ordinary and simple tests."[17]

Cardozo's theory did not gain general currency until the 1950s, when law professor William L. Prosser argued that people harmed by goods they bought did not need privity (contractual relations) with the products' manufacturers to sue for damages. Strict liability gained support within the academic community and began to appear in other state court decisions. But the defective automobile wheel began the modern concept of products liability, a concept that now dominates the field of tort liability, an example of punctuated equilibrium in which a novel court decision bided its time until the occasion came for it to replace older precedent. The origin of mass products liability and the modernization of strict liability for products defects all would grow from a single broken tire, but the evolution was not a steady and gradual one.[18]

One more example shows that the evolution of law in the punctuated equilibrium model does not result in the end of change, but instead redirects it. Consider the constitutionalization of the right of privacy. Today, personal liberties like the right to reproductive choice and the right to engage in sexual activities with same-sex partners rest upon the right of privacy the High Court found in the Constitution. But that right was not always there. It began in a small place, a kind of legal backwater, with unwanted photographs of a wedding. Intrusive photographers at the wedding of Louis Brandeis's law partner Samuel Warren had taken pictures, and these a newspaper had published. In 1890, Brandeis and Warren wrote an article for the *Harvard Law Review* arguing that privacy did not require physical invasion (trespass) on another person's land. "The right to life has come to mean the right to enjoy life,—the right to be let alone; the right to liberty secures the exercise of extensive civil privileges; and the term 'property' has grown to comprise every form of possession— intangible, as well as tangible." Brandeis argued as if the law was evolving toward a purer form, a progress of sensitivity.

This development of the law was inevitable. The intense intellectual and emotional life, and the heightening of sensations which came with the advance of civilization, made it clear to men that only a part of the pain, pleasure, and profit of life lay in physical things. Thoughts, emotions, and sensations demanded legal recognition, and the beautiful capacity for growth which characterizes the common law enabled the judges to afford the requisite protection, without the interposition of the legislature.

Actually, the law had not yet arrived at this place, and Brandeis's case was quite novel. So he backtracked a little: "For years there has been a feeling that the law must afford some remedy for the unauthorized circulation of portraits of private persons; and the evil of invasion of privacy by the newspapers. . . . Of the desirability—indeed of the necessity—of some such protection, there can, it is believed, be no doubt. The press is overstepping in every direction the obvious bounds of propriety and of decency." But the law did not provide a remedy—not yet.[19]

The constitutional enunciation of the right of privacy came seventy-five years after Brandeis and Warren made their plea. In *Griswold v. Connecticut* (1965), the state's family planning advocates finally got the U.S. Supreme Court to hear their appeal against Connecticut laws banning the dissemination of birth control information. Under the obscenity laws, a doctor could not offer advice on birth control to a patient. Planned Parenthood began its battle against the state's old (1879) birth control law in the 1930s, but for thirty years neither the state courts nor the state legislature would budge.

In 1961, Estelle Griswold, appointed head of Connecticut Planned Parenthood in 1954, arranged for a married couple seeking counseling and a doctor providing it at the Planned Parenthood clinic to be prosecuted under the law. It was a test case arranged so that the parties could appeal what they knew would be conviction under the state law. She and the doctor appealed their conviction to the state courts and thence to the U.S. Supreme Court, the appeal aided by the American Civil Liberties Union and Planned Parenthood of America. The Court heard the case and decided it for the petitioners. Justice William O. Douglas wrote for the majority:

> The Bill of Rights have penumbras, formed by emanations from those guarantees that help give them life and substance. . . . Various guarantees create zones of privacy. The right of association contained in the penumbra of the First Amendment is one. . . . The Third Amendment in its prohibition against the quartering of soldiers "in any house" in time of peace without the consent of the owner is another facet of that privacy. The Fourth Amendment explicitly affirms the "right of the people to be secure in their persons, houses, papers, and effects, against unreasonable searches and seizures." The Fifth Amendment in its Self-Incrimination Clause enables the citizen to create a zone of privacy which government may not force him to surrender to his detriment. The Ninth Amendment provides: "The enumeration in the Constitution, of certain rights, shall not be construed to deny or disparage others retained by the people."

From that case and opinion came a slew of right-to-privacy decisions, including the right to terminate a pregnancy (*Roe v. Wade* [1973]) and the right to choose a sexual partner (*Lawrence v. Texas* [2003]).[20]

Some of the most important and novel new species of legal thinking and action arose in what had been backwaters of law, and finding themselves without much competition where they were, spread to larger pools. There the new ideas, well suited to a changed legal environment, gained attention and adherents.

Whether they survive depends, of course, on what new ideas are now crawling out of isolated, brackish pools of law and lurching toward mainstreams.

## Selfish Memes

The third evolutionary model that might be deployed to narrate the path of the law proposes that ideas of law survive when they are surrounded by supportive ideas in other fields of thought. Consider, for example, the idea of private property. The liberty of which the framers spoke was the liberty to own, acquire, and dispose of private property, saving it from a grasping or corrupt state. As John Adams wrote, "the moment the idea is admitted into society that property is not as sacred as the laws of God and there is not the force of law and public justice to protect it, anarchy and tyranny commence." The presumption is still there. As Frank Michelman, the doyen of property law professors, conceded in 1988, "The founders of American constitutionalism did indeed rely on the idea of a rule of law—of politically transcendent norms and methods for elaborating them—for the reconciliation of popular sovereignty with limited government. Moreover, property was their inspiration for the idea of a private sphere of individual self-determination securely bounded off from politics by law."[21]

Indeed, one of the major formative roles of the state was to protect the property of those who had wealth against the demands of those who did not. When the have-nots decided to protest against the control of the new states by the haves in Shays' Rebellion (Massachusetts, 1786–1787), the Whiskey Rebellion (Pennsylvania and Maryland, 1793–1794), or Fries Rebellion (Pennsylvania, 1798–1799), state governments formed in revolution had no compunction about pursuing and jailing the men who served in the revolutionary armies. The original purpose of urban police forces was to protect the homes, businesses, and person of the well-to-do against the "dangerous classes," a nineteenth-century term for the poor. As Charles Loring Brace, a leading Victorian Era philanthropist and founder of the private foster care movement, wrote in 1872, "the class of a city most dangerous to its property, its morals and its political life, are the ignorant, destitute, untrained and abandoned youth: the outcast street children grown up to be voters, to be the implements of demagogues, the 'feeders' of criminals, and the sources of domestic outbreaks and violations of law." Brace wanted the dangerous classes brought up to understand the sanctity of private property. He was concerned that government not deal with the problems of street crime or urban poverty by redistributing wealth. He opposed strikes by unions and organized protests in favor of wealth sharing according to the "natural laws" of capital.[22]

What happens to such a legal idea when its supporting notions begin to change? When it becomes isolated and finds itself surrounded by antipathetical notions? Brace knew that private property was not sacred in America, not in 1872, and even more so today. The state can restrict property uses through zoning; take by taxing personal, corporate, and real property; and through eminent domain and confiscation deploy powerful tools to reconfigure property use. The state can redistribute wealth by using tax monies or other funds to subsidize public education, health, and safety. Advocates of greater redistribution have argued that housing and employment should be subsidized as well. Michelman again:

> The bounding of entitlements, however, could not forever remain conceptually and morally obvious, apolitical work. Changed and intensified modes of social interaction dislodged latent complexity and so gave rise to the disintegrative analytical vocabulary, and practice in its use, that enables us today to talk so easily and compellingly

about conceptual severance. Such changes, along with the emergence of the economically active and regulatory state with its licenses, franchises, and the like, pushed towards the denaturalization and positivization (implying the politicization) of property. Progressives and legal realists came on the scene to demonstrate how in modern conditions the prime moral and political values associated with property—independence, security, privacy—are as much defeated as they are served by adherence to a highly formal system of highly abstract property rights. There is synergy among these effects. For example, the better we learn the analytical lesson of conceptual severance—that every particle of legally sanctioned advantage is property—the more we are forced to recognize in every act of government a redefinition and adjustment of a property boundary. The war between popular self-government and strongly constitutionalized property now comes to seem not containable but total.[23]

The legal meme is a replicator. It makes more memes like itself. The legal idea that can no longer perform this function for whatever reason will find itself in the waste bin of legal history. It has lost the evolutionary battle to reproduce itself. But that battle continues among those memes that have survived. The battle seems to have no end. The paths of the law continue to diverge. Critical legal studies' adherents call this the indeterminacy of law, an incomplete evolution marked by its "gaps" and "ambiguities." Fair enough, but a better description might be the selfish gene evolution of law.[24]

The law today is profoundly different in many areas than it was at the founding of the nation. The nation of laws is a nation of changing laws. Whether one portrays those changes as evolutionary or not, whether one sees distinct stages or not, whether the progress or the continuing oppositions seems the more striking, no one can deny that change has been profound. Racism, once enshrined in local law, is now contained, if not eradicated, by equal opportunity law. Statutes and case law are driving sex discrimination, once routinely countenanced, from businesses and schools.

But change may only shift the ground on which advocates of law do battle. The right to an abortion and the right to live with a partner of one's choice are not settled matters. Indeed, nothing is more contentious in American law today than the battle between "choice" and "right to life," except, perhaps, the battle over same-sex marriages. The battle over government takings for the purpose of redistributive programs like Social Security and national health care has changed its terminology but not its principles. What the law does is transform the struggle for survival—for wealth and power—into one for legal privilege and duty.

American law not only channels and controls these struggles; it is itself transformed by contests. It is enriched. Law in the Darwinian model of progress gains by competition; law in a punctuated equilibrium model of progress can find new means of expressing itself; and law in a memetic model gives shape and form to the values in the surrounding society.

There is one essential piece of the Darwinian schema of change missing from the analogy drawn here between biological and legal evolution. Darwin posited that the agent of change was random mutation. Legal change is not random, but conscious, indeed self-conscious. For a nation of laws is also a nation of people, and it is the participation of people in the legal process that gives energy and meaning to the law's evolution. These people are the law's adversaries and partisans.

# 3

## *Adversaries and Partisans*

As the opening words of the preamble to the federal Constitution, "we the people of the United States," remind Americans, everyone in the country is affected by law. No simple phrase better conveys the concept of nation of laws in a democratic context. For we the people are not just the object of the laws, we are vitally involved in the making of laws. Ordinary people can go to law and make a difference in how all of us are treated. Lawsuits against tobacco companies and settlements of potential litigation have reshaped public financing of hospitals and care of the elderly. A family upset with a school district suspending their children for wearing black armbands to protest the Vietnam War can expand the entire idea of free speech. A woman who sues her former employer for employment discrimination when she refused to engage in sex with a superior can create a new cause of action called hostile work environment. A homeowner jailed for owning pornographic literature after an illegal police search can appeal her case all the way to the High Court and extend the protections against warrantless searches.[1]

A nation of laws is not simply doctrines, rules, opinions, courts, legislatures, and practices. Instead, it is people behaving in certain recognizable ways. It is an institution that allows people to settle grievances, plan for the future, or simply gain recognition for their views. But widespread participation of Americans in the legal process does more for the nation of laws than democratize the process—it profoundly changes the process. A law imposed from the top down, from a king even as wise as Solon or Solomon, may be just, but it limits access to the law. A people's law creates many access points.

The democratic nature of American law also underscores one of the unique characteristics of participation. For the law in America depends upon adversarial process—me against you, my lawyer against yours. The macroscopic view of this kind of adversarial process is politics itself, my interests and policy aims versus yours played out on the stage of local, state, and national politics. Adversarial politics enters law through the legislatures and the courts. Even legal education is adversarial and partisan. For the professors do not stand aloof from the contests and controversies of law. Instead, they plunge right in, adding their voices to the clamor for reform or retrenchment. So many people acting in an adversarial and partisan capacity should have led to a perpetual train wreck. Instead, granting some latitude, the trains of American law run on time.

## Litigants and Jurors—Law from the Bottom Up

The most numerous adversaries in American legal history are the men and women who go to law to vindicate their rights, force others to perform their obligations, or find themselves in court as defendants. They are the pawns in the chess game of adversarial pleading. What turns an ordinary person into a glazed-eye, fire-breathing litigant? A study of litigation in early America argued that a surge in litigation came when older face-to-face obligations were replaced by arms-length commercial relations. People who had, in previous years, trusted other people to do the right thing became furious when it seemed that those same people were breaking the rules. Plaintiffs sued when they thought that defendants were no longer trustworthy. Defendants refused to settle out of court because they thought that plaintiffs had become unreasonable. It was a breakdown of the common understandings in these dealings that caused the rise in litigation. "Litigation ceased to be the last chapter in a communal story and became the introduction to a detached, abstract legal episode."[2]

Years of my own conversations with litigators suggest that the same reasons that motivated people to go to law in the eighteenth century remain potent motivators today. It is all about broken promises, wounded pride, damaged honor, and the desire for vengeance. Parties who go to law often have an advantage over newcomers. Plaintiffs are often of higher socioeconomic status than defendants. Businesses are more likely to sue than customers.[3]

Litigants come to court to "tell their story." The litigation forces the other party to listen to the story and reply. The irony of this desire is that the story the court will permit the litigant to tell is framed not by the litigant's own sense of what was important or what went wrong, but by rules of evidence that seem arbitrary and strained to most litigants. Still, the opportunity is "cathartic," the court a place where justice may simply mean the chance to be heard.[4]

Anecdotal evidence asserts that "litigation fever" is always on the rise, something like the inchoate but unshakeable conviction that street crime is worse than ever, the breakup of the American family is accelerating, and sexual promiscuity multiplies every day. But there is no evidence of a connection between a "litigation explosion" and the implosion of American values. In fact, litigation is not an avalanche, an epidemic, or any other kind of disaster or disease running wild.[5]

The ordinary American is not only a potential litigant. He or she is also a potential grand juror or trial juror. The grand jury is an institution that goes back to medieval England. In its inception, the role of the grand jurors was to inform the court what had happened in the vicinity based on their own knowledge. Twenty-four were summoned from each county by the judges to report on crimes and identify the culprits. By the fourteenth century, the grand jury lost that function and took on another, hearing and weighing evidence that their neighbors had violated a criminal law.

The "true bill" of the grand jury sent the defendant in cases of serious crime to trial before another kind of jury, the little (petite) or trial jury of "twelve good men and true" drawn from the vicinity of the sitting court. In its inception, again in medieval England, the trial jury verdict replaced tests of truth by combat, ordeal, and compurgation. The last of these tests required parties to produce twelve neighbors to swear to the truth of the party's claims. The crown offered the trial jury to the defendant as an alternative, for a fee. The independence of the trial jury's verdict, that is, the jury's finding of fact, was established by the seventeenth century's end. The American colonists put great store by the trial jury, regarding it as one of the basic features of the common law they inherited from England. They rarely called for it in civil suits (it cost too much), but the trial jury was the bulwark of criminal procedure in cases of serious crime.

In the early republic, jurors were drawn from lists of property holders. Thus the jury represented the better sort of members of society. Women were not called to sit on juries, though they might stand before a jury as a party to a suit or a criminal defendant. When jury duty was tied to voter registration in the twentieth century, however, women were called to jury duty. In 1927, Burnita Shelton Matthews reported on the progress of women in the jury box:

As early as 1911, Washington removed her ban on women jurors and Kansas did likewise in 1912. The laws in some states declare that a person qualified to vote is also qualified for jury duty. So as soon as women were accorded the right to vote in such states, their right to serve on juries, as a general rule, was automatically established. That was what happened in Nevada in 1914, in Michigan in 1918, and in Delaware, Indiana, Iowa, Kentucky, Ohio and Pennsylvania in 1920. On the other hand, it was by specific enactments that women were qualified for the jury in California in 1917, and in Arkansas, Louisiana, Maine, Minnesota, New Jersey, North Dakota, Oregon and Wisconsin, in 1921.

Women could, however, opt out of the jury pool at will until the 1970s in most jurisdictions. Some lawyers did not trust the new jurors. The first woman called for jury duty in California, Josephine Anna Engelman, was seated in the pool but was removed on a peremptory challenge by the plaintiff's lawyer for being a woman.[6]

The modern jury pool is somewhat older, better educated, and a little more wealthy than the general population because it is based on voter registration and driver's license holding. The pool is representative of racial diversity and gender, but not in proportion to the general population in the jurisdiction. Lawyers may "strike" (exclude) jurors for cause, for example, when the juror knows one of the parties, has an interest in the case, or knows one of the counsel. Counsel have as well a set number of peremptory (arbitrary) strikes. No juror may be struck because of his or her race, religion, or other personal characteristic, but they may be struck if they have already arrived at a decision on the matter at hand.

In early America, juries retired for a very short time to deliberate and reach a verdict. They might even be polled where they sat in the jury box. This was because trials rarely took more than a few hours. Today a major trial may consume weeks or months of a juror's time. For this reason, alternative jurors may be chosen to prevent a mistrial when a juror is unable to continue. Well into the twentieth century local court parties often knew the jurors and the jurors knew one another. Although the judge always instructed the jury on the law, and they were to try "well and impartially," their local knowledge and their impression of the parties in court was a part of their fact finding. Modern jurors are not likely to know one another, particularly in big cities, and personal knowledge plays a lesser role. There are exceptions to this rule, however. After they had announced their verdict of not guilty, the jurors in the murder trial of O. J. Simpson admitted that they were influenced by their prior impressions of Los Angeles Police Department misconduct regarding people of color.[7]

Make no mistake, though instructed to simply render verdicts on matters of fact, jurors are full partners in the adversarial process. How the jury sees evidence is no more important than how the jury sees the defendant and the plaintiff or the prosecutor. Dress, demeanor, and a thousand other cues echoing in the jurors' own experience go from jury box to jury room when the jurors retire to deliberate. The law may be blind in the abstract, but jurors see what they want to see because they are part of the general population.

When, for example, a criminal trial becomes a newsworthy event, lay people invest tremendous emotional energy in its outcome. Because they have participated in trials themselves, they identify with protagonists in the courtroom. During the O. J. Simpson murder trial, observers split along racial lines in their view of the conduct of the trial, the prosecution, and the defense. Sitting with students at Harvard Law School when the verdict was announced, one law student reported that students of color cheered while white students were stunned and angry. Much of the country divided the same way. A democratic, participatory law cannot escape feeling the conflicts that divide the nation as a whole when adversaries fill the courtroom.[8]

Whether suer or sued, grand juror or trial juror, today the ordinary American has more direct experience with the law, and takes a more prominent part in its outcomes, than in past times. Because of the mass participatory character of American law, the operation of law is more democratic here than anywhere else in the world. When the trial of a celebrity or a politician makes the news, millions of Americans become virtual jurors, judges, and lawyers.

## Lawyers

Lawyering in America is a profession, an occupation, a business, and for some, a calling. It is a profession because practicing requires a license. The license, in turn, comes with rigorous training and examinations. It is an occupation because it demands time and application. It is a business because lawyers are paid for their services. It is a calling—for some—because it brings out their courage, faith, and adherence to principle. But lawyers are like the people they represent, eager adversaries. The greatest lawyers are competitive champions of their causes, reveling in victory over an opponent.

Lawyers are revered and reviled, the first person one calls when one is in trouble with the law and among the lowest-rated of all the professions in every public opinion poll. Ambrose Bierce's *The Devil's Dictionary* (originally published in 1906 as *The Cynic's Wordbook*) defined a lawyer as "one skilled in circumvention of the law." As lawyer Fred Rodell wrote many years ago,

> In tribal times there were the medicine men. In the middle ages, there were the priests. Today there are the lawyers.

For every age, a group of bright boys, learned in their trades and jealous of their learning, who blend technical competence with plain and fancy hocus-pocus to make themselves masters of their fellow men. For every age, a pseudo-intellectual autocracy, guarding the tricks of its trade from the uninitiated, and running, after its own pattern, the civilization of the day.[9]

Rodell's overly broad satire still reflects an important truth. Lawyers' importance in the politics of the new nation cannot be overstated. As Alexis de Tocqueville, an aristocratic French visitor to America, observed in 1830, "One must not believe, furthermore, that in the United States the spirit of the lawyer is uniquely confined within the precincts of the courts; it extends well beyond." The first two generations of American national history were blessed with battalions of great lawyers. Most of them gravitated as if by natural attraction to politics. Jefferson, John Adams, and Alexander Hamilton were lawyers. So were Andrew Jackson, John C. Calhoun, Henry Clay, and Daniel Webster. The same abilities and values that made them able lawyers made them successful politicians: a canny sense of the law, a willingness to work hard, and a belief in themselves.

Lawyers played a vital enabling role in the nation's commercial and industrial growth. Professionals in a nation that early on respected professionalism, they occupied a special niche. They were also the target of broad caricature and serious criticism long before Rodell lambasted them. For as America became more democratic, the lawyers more and more resembled an elite club whose members alone understood what they called the "science" of law (and its increasing complexity). Their jousting for fees also put them in a bad light. From the first, lawyering in America exhibited the same ambiguities as American law.[10]

Local bar associations, dating from the colonial period, were hardly professional in modern terms. Their purpose was to ensure that anyone who hung out a shingle had some minimal competence. Would-be lawyers were examined by a panel of judges before they could practice before the colonial supreme courts. Family and clientage influenced these hearings. Patrick Henry studied for the bar a few months then passed his exam—the examiners were his relatives and his relatives' friends. Judges often knew little more than these lawyers, and the entire crew—judges, a clerk, the lawyers—traveled about from courthouse to courthouse. Clients trailed along or waited for the procession to appear to have their legal business settled.

In the closing years of the antebellum era, the legal profession was changing. Forcing and shaping the change was the growing profusion of law books. Massachusetts' Joseph Story and New York's James Kent among other jurists had written extensive treatises on American law. The states were now publishing *Reports*—yearly collations of the opinions of their appeals courts. Law book sales and the size of individual lawyers' and bar association's libraries had grown apace. A new species of publisher had appeared, catering profitably to the legal trade. American law books, published in America, were squeezing the English law books off the lawyers' shelves (although American publishers were also reprinting and selling contemporary English treatises). Even used law books commanded a good price—shades of the immense expense of law books (and subscriptions to online services like Lexis and Westlaw) today.

Lawyers played vital roles on both sides of the Mason-Dixon line during the Civil War. Government lawyers oversaw large-scale confiscation programs in both sections. Lawyers filled key administrative roles in the burgeoning bureaucracies the war spurred. In the U.S. Congress, lawyers led the way in framing the Reconstruction Amendments to the Constitution and the postwar reconstruction program. One artifact of this was the creation of the Department of Justice in Washington, D.C., in 1871.

After the Civil War, the legal profession divided into elite and nonelite streams. More than 95 percent of the 40,000 or so practitioners continued to read law or attend a year or two of law school and then stand for the bar. But newly formed city bar associations were demanding more of their members than the state bar associations. A study of the Chicago bar revealed that only 12 percent of those who began practicing in the Civil War era had attended law schools, while by 1915 nearly 90 percent had graduated from law schools.[11]

In the major cities, individual practice was giving way to partnerships, and some lawyers were beginning to specialize in especially lucrative fields of lawyering, representing railroad and industrial enterprises. These men (very few women were allowed to practice law) began to see themselves not simply as the better-paid portion of the profession, but as the upholders of the highest standards of law practice. In 1878, Yale law professor Simeon Baldwin called 100 "leading men" and men of "high promise" to the resort spa of Saratoga Springs, New York, to found an American Bar Association. The first constitution of the ABA promised "the advancement of the science of jurisprudence, the promotion of the administration of justice and a uniformity of legislation throughout the country." In fact, the ABA sought a stable profession controlled by its elite members. No Jews, African Americans, or women were asked to join. Thirty years later, the ABA still admitted to membership fewer than 10 percent of the nation's lawyers.[12]

In the first years of the twentieth century, wealthy businessmen were the most visible and the most trusted spokesmen for American values. It was the heyday of Andrew Carnegie, John D. Rockefeller, Henry Ford, Thomas Alva Edison, and J. P. Morgan. But two lawyers, as different in outlook and career as possible, one a perennial outsider, the other a consummate insider, one the advocate of workingmen's rights, the other a defender of corporate capitalism, were just as prominent as the moguls of the marketplace. Tireless advocates in the courtroom, they epitomized the adversarial essence of lawyering.

Clarence Darrow was an outsider by choice. Always confident, sometimes prickly, a radical at heart, he found in the underdog a cause always worth defending. Darrow was born in 1857 in an Ohio hamlet, the son of an abolitionist father and feminist mother. Clarence followed in their footsteps, capable of great empathy with those who sorrowed, those in need, and those neglected by the powerful. Darrow would have lived out his life as a moderately successful local lawyer and politician had he not decided to chance his fortunes in Chicago in 1887. It was a year after the city had exploded in labor violence, and Darrow saw his calling as defending the organizers of labor. He represented Eugene V. Debs when he and the rest of the leadership of the American Railway Union violated a federal court injunction against the union's sympathy strike in the Pullman car company case. Darrow spoke for socialists and anarchists in free-speech cases; for "Big Bill" Haywood, the leader of the International Workers of the World in a 1907 murder case; and for the United Mine Workers when they went on strike in 1903.

Darrow understood that the primary role of lawyers in America was to act as counsel for clients. Lawyers are allowed some latitude in their "zealous advocacy" of their client's interest. In the words of the American Bar Association *Model Code of Professional Responsibility* (1908 and after) and the *Model Rules of Professional Conduct* (2004): "As a representative of clients, a lawyer performs various functions. As advisor, a lawyer provides a client with an informed understanding of the client's legal rights and obligations and explains their practical implications. As advocate, a lawyer zealously asserts the client's position under the rules of the adversary system."

But how far can a lawyer go in his or her zealous advocacy? In the early morning of October 1, 1910, the *Los Angeles Times* building exploded. Fifty people were killed by the dynamite laid by three union radicals. The *Times* was rabidly antiunion, but defenders of organized labor denied that union men were responsible, and they hired Darrow to defend James and John McNamara, who were accused of the crime. Darrow wavered. On the one hand, he knew that he might be defending two guilty men. On the other hand, he understood why men were driven to violence when injustice was palpable and lawful remedy unavailable. Still, he had "forebodings that I could not quiet."[13]

Darrow decided to plea bargain for the McNamaras. They confessed to the bombing, denying that they intended to hurt anyone in the building. Labor turned its back on them and on Darrow. Worse was to come. Darrow had an associate find out all he could about the prospective jurors in the case before it went to trial. The associate was accused of attempting to bribe one of the members of the jury panel. After the McNamaras were sentenced, the prosecution indicted Darrow for directing the alleged bribery attempt. A hung jury followed by an acquittal saved Darrow from prison, but not before Darrow pleaded with the jury: "I am on trial [for bribery] because I am a lover of the poor, a friend of the oppressed, because I have stood by labor for all these years, and have brought down upon my head the wrath of the criminal interests in the country."[14]

Though in the coming years he won more than his share of the great cases—saving Richard Leopold and Nathan Loeb from the gallows, defending black homeowner Ossian Sweet from a murder charge, and making a mockery of the antievolution arguments at the trial of John Scopes—Darrow remained the maverick loner, facing down all odds. In death as in life, Darrow embodied the contrary natures of American law. Though he had once been a wealthy man, he died in 1938, nearly penniless, in a Chicago rented room. But he got the last word—his eulogy, delivered by a long-time friend, was the same he gave at the death of his beloved mentor, lawyer and reformer John Peter Altgeld.[15]

John W. Davis of West Virginia, the insider, rarely spoke for the underdog. He believed that the lawyer's purpose was to protect the best interests of the better sort of people. He was called the lawyer's lawyer for good reason. A member of Congress from West Virginia, appointed an Ambassador to Great Britain by president Woodrow Wilson, a Democratic candidate for the presidency in 1924, and partner in one of the foremost Washington, D.C., law firms in the twentieth century, Davis was never far from the centers of power. His courtly manners, his powers of oratory, and his meticulousness in preparation made him a formidable adversary and an advocate his clients trusted in the courtroom. He argued 140 cases before the High Court, a modern record, and was so respected there that the justices rarely interrupted his oral argument.

His upbringing did not herald such greatness. Davis was born in 1875 in West Virginia. His father was a local lawyer and politician. The family was not wealthy. Davis did not have the finances to attend law school until he earned enough teaching school. But he so impressed his teachers at Washington and Lee Law School that upon his graduation they offered him a post on the faculty.

Though a lifelong Democrat, he was a conservative at heart. He opposed big government and espoused the states' rights philosophy of limited federal government intervention in states' affairs. He opposed giving women and African Americans the vote and voted against the federal antilynching laws and later civil rights legislation. Battling against New Deal regulations, he and his firm represented the largest corporations in the country.

The very last of his cases became his most famous. His client was the state of South Carolina, and at stake was the state's segregation of elementary schools. In *Briggs v. Elliott*, black residents of Clarendon County, a rural area north of Charleston, had at first asked the state to provide buses for their elementary school–age children. White children were bused to their schools, while black children had to find other means of transportation. The black schools were woefully underfunded and ill kept, compared to the white schools. From 1947, when the first suit was filed, until 1951, when the NAACP's legal defense fund appealed the state court's decisions upholding segregation to the federal courts, the state refused to concede an inch to the black parents. In the meantime, the parents who brought the suit were harassed and threatened by their white neighbors.

When the federal courts agreed to hear the case, the state shifted its ground and promised to equalize funding for the two school systems under the doctrine of "separate but equal" enunciated in *Plessy v. Ferguson* (1896). Governor James F. Byrnes, who had briefly served on the High Court, introduced a bill to this effect in the state legislature, but it was apparent to all that the promise of equalization was a sham designed to prevent the Court from deciding against the state. Such bad faith by state officials was already commonplace in civil rights suits.

South Carolina would not abandon its Jim Crow school system quietly, however. Byrnes asked Davis to represent the state when the lower federal courts' decisions were appealed to the U.S. Supreme Court, in 1952. Davis truly believed in South Carolina's cause and that blacks were inferior to whites. Thus both races benefited from separate schools. As he wrote to Byrnes, on December 23, 1952: "It is not inconceivable that in addition to anatomical differences [between whites and blacks] there are also differences in the intellectual processes, in tastes and aptitudes?"[16]

On December 17, 1953, Davis argued South Carolina's case before the Court. He was confident that he would prevail. Segregation was well established in southern communities and often in the past approved by the High Court (though a series of recent cases had found that segregation of professional schools violated the Equal Protection Clause of the Fourteenth Amendment). Davis opined, "Somewhere, some time, to every principle there comes a moment of repose when it has been so often pronounced, so confidently relied upon, so long continued, that it passes the limits of judicial discretion and disturbance." With tears in his eyes, his emotion and his frailty apparent to everyone on the bench, Davis concluded that black children would not benefit from desegregation. He died shortly after a unanimous Court found South Carolina's segregated system unconstitutional.[17]

One can find dozens more pairings of opposites like Darrow and Davis—Hamilton and Jefferson; Jefferson and Marshall; Webster and Calhoun; Lincoln and Douglas; Stephen J. Field and John Marshall Harlan—and for every famous lawyer in American history there are thousands who live and work in relative obscurity. Practicing in small cities and towns, working alone or in partnerships of two to five lawyers, they are the bedrock of the profession. Throughout American history these attorneys at law mirrored the characteristics of their neighbors. Antebellum southern lawyers aspired to gentility and bought plantations. Wild West "cowtown" lawyers were rough-and-ready brawlers.

Today local lawyers are allowed to advertise their services, and the "yellow pages" are filled with their business: representing clients in automobile accidents, DUI, wrongful death suits and workers' compensation litigation, divorce and child custody, bankruptcy and debt relief, and criminal defense. Real estate law is another staple of "general practice."

Major trends in the second half of the twentieth century include the opening of general practice to women and ethnic minorities. Indeed, the growing proportion of women lawyers in the profession has been the most striking demographic change in lawyering in the twentieth century. Women from the outset understood that advocacy was not limited to the courtroom. They had to argue themselves into the profession. The first of the women lawyers, Clara Shortridge Foltz of California, was famous for her sharp-tongued ripostes. "Counsel intimates with a curl on his lip that I am called the lady lawyer. I am sorry I cannot return the compliment, but I cannot. I never heard anybody call him any kind of lawyer at all." In the first half of the twentieth century, most women lawyers worked in sole practice, if they were able to practice law at all. Marriage and career were rivals, with the latter usually losing out. In the 1950s, the prognosis was mixed. Women did "the legal work believed appropriate for women—namely family and government law, public interest and defender work." Sandra Day O'Connor, a future Supreme Court justice, recalled that she could not find a job with a major law firm after she graduated near the top of her class from Stanford Law School. In fact, the only job offer was as "a legal secretary." Today, women comprise a significant minority of lawyers (exceeding over 30 percent of the total), and they are a majority of graduating law students in the major law schools. They do not earn, as a group, as much as male lawyers, but the gap is closing. At one time discriminated against in gaining the coveted partnership in large law firms, they are slowly closing that gap as well, and now comprise nearly 20 percent of the partners in large firms. When controlled for age and experience, the gender gap in the rewards for male and female lawyers closes further.[18]

Minority members of the legal profession are so common as to be almost unnoticeable. The National Bar Association is a professional organization for African American lawyers and the Hispanic National Bar Association represents Latinos in the legal profession. The American Bar Association has African American and Hispanic leaders as well. Fred Alvarez, head of the ABA's Commission on Racial and Ethnic Diversity in the Profession, explained:

> The ABA Commission on Racial and Ethnic Diversity in the Profession is a diverse group of committed lawyers that, through its work and programs, is the catalyst for

creating leadership and economic opportunities for racially
and ethnically diverse lawyers within the ABA and the
legal profession. We provide a voice to surface and tackle
issues of discrimination, racism and bigotry, and to inspire
the ABA and the profession to value differences, to be
sensitive to prejudice, and to reflect the society they serve.

Local bar associations are no longer exclusive white men's clubs.
Legal aid societies provide counsel for the poor. Corporate practice in the larger firms (and these had grown to thousands of
lawyers by the end of the twentieth century) continued to attract
the graduates of the top law schools, but public service law, special interest group advocacy, and government lawyering were
also attractive, and some law schools reduced or forgave tuition
for graduates entering public interest law practice. The American
Civil Liberties Union, founded in 1916, has over 500,000 members and litigating affiliates in every state. Representing clients
whose causes may be unpalatable to most Americans, from
Communists to neo-Nazis, "The ACLU is our nation's guardian
of liberty, working daily in courts, legislatures and communities
to defend and preserve the individual rights and liberties that the
Constitution and laws of the United States guarantee everyone
in this country." The Legal Defense Fund of the National Association for the Advancement of Colored People, and more
recently, the National Organization of Women, employ lawyers.
So does Ralph Nader's "Raiders," a consumer advocacy coalition.[19]

Of whatever background and inclination, entering the profession from whatever direction and with whatever values the
lawyers might have, lawyers have become more and more
important parts of our lives. The nation of laws could not function without the nation's lawyers. Indeed, the chambers of our
legislatures would be empty without the participation of lawyers.
But the public interest lawyer, the minority lawyer, and the

lawyer of lost causes are still adversarial participants in a system that rewards the successful advocate and his or her client.

## *Legislators—The People's Representatives*

The founders of the American nation agreed that the most important branch of government in the new states must be the legislative. An executive could become corrupt and overweaning. Courts were, at least in theory, limited to the adjudication of particular cases involving the parties coming before them. The legislature represented the sovereignty of the people. The nation's most important laws would be statutes.

Over time, the history of voting for state legislatures and Congress has become even more representative of all the people, as bars to voting by women, minorities, and the poor have fallen away. But while the making of law in a legislature requires some degree of collaborative compromise and concession, allowing different groups to find some common ground, legislatures are representative bodies and the groups and interests they represent vie for the same piece of the public pie. Even a "do-nothing Congress" is a hotbed of partisanship.[20]

The adversarial style of litigation and lawyering makes its way into the legislative chamber. That is why our statutes are so detailed and so often riddled with amendments, riders, and extraneous matter. Legislators represent constituencies in a fashion parallel to the way that counsel represents clients. In the legislature, politics (the macroscopic version of contest) replaces adversarial process (the microscopic, individualized version of contest).

The demographic and occupational makeup of the state legislatures, and to a lesser extent Congress, reflects this cross-fertilization of adversarial process from the courtroom to the assembly hall. For example, the state of Georgia has 178 assembly members, and, in 2009, 26 of them listed their occupation as attorney or lawyer. The lawyers are closely followed by the real estate agents and the businessmen and businesswomen. Insurance agents came in fourth, followed by retired schoolteachers, ministers, motivational speakers, college professors, and car dealership owners. The Georgia Senate has 56 seats. In 2009, 12 of them were filled by lawyers. The same pattern can be found throughout the country. The legislatures represent the distribution of business and professional occupations in the state, skewed in favor of law-related jobs. The pattern of occupation in Congress makes the pattern even clearer. In 2006, 53 percent of the U.S. Senate seats were occupied by lawyers. Over one-third of the members of the House of Representatives were lawyers.[21]

For some critics, the number of lawyers in the legislative branch of government seems excessive. Why should they dominate the list of occupations? Conspiratorial thinkers have an answer—the lawyers have a vested interest in keeping the law a mystery that only lawyers can solve. That is the reason why some acts of Congress run to hundreds of pages of highly complicated and technically sophisticated language. Another answer seems more rational—Congress is a lawmaking body. Would anyone argue that the courts should be staffed by nonlawyers?[22]

In fact the lawyers are fleeing the legislatures. As the *New York Times* reported in 1999,

> state legislatures have always had their farmers, teachers, engineers and entrepreneurs, but from the early days of the Republic, no group has been as over-represented as lawyers. But for the last three decades, even as the profession has grown in numbers, its grip on state capitols has steadily slipped, a trend that continued in the turnover brought by the November elections. In states with the big cities that have high concentrations of lawyers, the drop has been especially pronounced. In 1969, 61 percent of New York's state legislators were lawyers; today, 34

percent are. In California, the figure has fallen to 22
percent from 48 percent 30 years ago.

Apparently legislating takes too much time from much more
lucrative law practice.[23]

Whoever is sitting in the legislature, bills do not easily
become law. In the first sessions of Congress in the twenty-first
century, an average of over 6,000 bills were introduced in the
House of Representatives each session, and fewer than 350
passed both houses and were signed into law by the president.
In 2005–2006, that number increased to 480 (not counting res-
olutions and private bills). Legislatures were more active in earlier years. Colonial assemblies made little distinction between
private bills, giving to a person or a group of persons some charter, grant, permission, or fee, and public bills, regulating prices
or announcing policy. The result was very busy sessions. In 1897,
the governor of New York complained that the assembly was
deluging him with bills. There were over 1,000 introduced, of
which over 100 had passed both houses. From 1901to 1903,
Congress passed 2,781acts. In the next session, that number had
increased to 4,041, and the next saw 6,940. Congress was the
home of the pork barrel, as the members pillaged the public
treasury to reward special interests throughout the land.[24]

Nineteenth-century legislative acts, in general, were not well
drafted. One commentator called them "an affront to common
sense." Another suggested that lawyers did not pay much attention to legislation. Apparently, most courts did not pay much
attention either until after the Civil War. Then treatises and, still
later, casebooks on statutory interpretation appeared. Today
most schools offer courses on statutory interpretation. At Harvard Law School, it is a required first-year course:

This course will introduce students to the world of
legislation, regulation and administration that creates and

defines so much of our legal order. At the same time, it will begin to teach students to think about processes and structures of government and how they influence and affect legal outcomes. The course will introduce students to, and include materials on, most or all of the following topics: the separation of powers; the legislative process; statutory interpretation; delegation and administrative agency practice; and regulatory tools and strategies. The course will naturally lead into, and enable students to get more out of, advanced courses in the 2L and 3L years, on legislation, administrative law, a wide range of regulatory subjects (e.g., environmental law, securities law, telecommunications law), and constitutional law.[25]

Nineteenth-century legislation was pretty straightforward, aiding the canal and later the railroad industries, establishing banks and schools, and otherwise distributing the public fisc to business interests. Fence law was also a favorite subject. Some states anticipated the civil rights concerns of the twentieth century. The Pennsylvania state legislature was the first to ban racial discrimination on streetcars, in 1867. In the twentieth century, the rules for interpretation of statutes became more controversial as state legislatures and Congress moved into the business of regulation. "The last fifty to eighty years have seen a fundamental change in American law. In this time we have gone from a legal system dominated by common law, divined by courts, to one in which statutes, enacted by legislatures, have become the primary source of law." Courts have responded to the shift by deferring to legislatures more often than not when economic regulation was the subject, but paying closer attention (so-called strict scrutiny) when the subject matter concerned due process and equal protection rights. Individual judges are still divided over whether legislative intent, as evidenced in hearings, floor debates, or the comments of sponsors of bills, should be consulted in interpreting the meaning of acts.[26]

Most legislation falls in the category of public bills, prospective in operation and applying equally to all persons. The principle behind this is "rule of law." Consolidated as a doctrine by the English jurist A. V. Dicey at the end of the nineteenth century, the notion was in context a rationalization for England extending its laws to its African and Asian colonies. Shorn of its imperial garb, the doctrine is still a mainstay of legislative jurisprudence: the legislature must not be a tyrant indifferent to the popular will or the established usages of the law. No person was above the law; all must obey it; and it should favor no man against another. The law must privilege individual rights and individual property above the requirements of the state, unless the state itself was in peril.[27]

The proliferation of statute law may be the most obvious landmark of the supremacy of the legislative branch in a nation of laws, but the existence of so many laws, some running to hundreds of pages of detail, exacerbates the law's inconsistencies. Worse, from the standpoint of rule of law, the growing importance of legislation means a greater role for partisanship in law. For legislators are all about politics, and politics is forever shifting. Politics opens doors to the advocates of special interests, lobbyists, for example, who have no interest in a coherent law. So called "ear-marks" and late night riders to bills having nothing to do with the substance of the bill, amendments that are designed to cripple legislation rather than empower it, all undermine the law's lucidity.

The most infamous case of an attempt to amend-to-death was the effort of southern senators opposed to the Civil Rights Act of 1964 to kill it with amendments. Ironically, that bit of malicious mischief became the basis for equal opportunities for women in the workplace and education. As firsthand accounts of the efforts of floor leaders Mike Mansfield and Everett Dirksen to find a way to pass the Civil Rights Act in 1964 demonstrate, legislation can be a crazy quilt cut by the one-eyed and sewed by the blind.[28]

## Judges and Judging

Judges and courts in America today both complement and contrast with legislators and their assemblies. For the role of the judge theoretically is the adjudication of cases brought before her and the provision of particular remedies to the parties in her court. The judge looks back; the legislator looks forward. The judge confines her ruling to particular cases, the legislature provides for the general welfare. The judge is learned in the law; the legislator need not be. The judge is above politics; politics is the legislator's lifeblood. But the history of American law demonstrates that this theoretical division of duties is not strictly followed. Indeed, it is a rebuttable presumption, an argument championed by the legal profession. As Morton Horwitz reminds us, "The desire to separate law and politics has always been a central aspiration of the American legal profession. . . . If law is simply a product of power or will, any special claims of the profession to determine the nature and scope of legal development is undermined."[29]

The colonial judge was a man of position and respect in his town or parish, sometimes its best-educated individual. He held other offices—member of the assembly, churchwarden, militia colonel, and the like. Thus he was simultaneously involved in both adjudication and policy making. He did not recuse himself from cases in which he had an interest, and there was no bar to multiple office holding.

For much of the colonial period, judges were not usually learned in the law and had, if anything, only a few books of legal forms and perhaps one of the "abridgments" of English law by topic or a guide to the duties of justices of the peace. But by the end of the colonial period, enough of the far more learned and technical English forms of law had arrived in the colonies to transform practice in the courts. The judges donned a wig and a robe like their English counterparts, but they still depended upon counsel to guide them through the increasingly arcane pathways of the law.

One reason that the colonial judicial system worked absent a learned bench was that the colonists abandoned the myriad of specialized courts one found in England and established a simple hierarchy of courts of general jurisdiction. At the bottom was the justice of the peace's court, from which appeal might be had to the courts of general sessions or the peace, and thence to the supreme courts of the colony. The first states adopted this system, and it is still true of their judiciaries, with trial courts, sometimes called superior courts, intermediate courts of appeal, and supreme courts.

The state court systems vary in their shape and size. New Jersey has more than 400 trial, tax, and appeals court judges. The single county of Alameda, California, encompassing much of the eastern side of San Francisco Bay, has 69 superior (trial) court judges. North Dakota district (trial) court judges total only 49. Some states elect judges, while in others initial election is followed by tenure during good behavior. State courts apply state law and the state's constitution to cases coming before them but are also allowed to apply federal law and the federal Constitution when appropriate. When parties in a state court are not both citizens of that state, either party may elect to remove the suit to a federal court on the basis of "diversity of citizenship." There was as well a dollar threshold for removing a suit from state to federal court—the amount in 1789 was $500, a hefty sum at that time. Today the amount in dispute must equal or exceed $75,000. In the late nineteenth and early twentieth century, this "removal" was especially favored by railroad companies seeking friendlier judges in the federal courts. State court judges tended to favor the plaintiffs, often local people injured by the trains.[30]

The federal Constitution created only the U.S. Supreme Court, but in the same Article III permitted Congress to establish such inferior courts as it deemed necessary. In the Judiciary Act of 1789, the first of many judiciary enactments, Congress created a two-tiered system of inferior courts—district courts over which a district judge presided and circuit courts held over five geographic regions with the district judge and a Supreme Court justice riding circuit. In 1891, Congress finally lifted the burden of riding circuit from the shoulders of the High Court bench, creating an intermediate level of circuit courts of appeals staffed by their own judges. The jurisdiction of the district, courts of appeal, and Supreme Court have also been revised, with the end result that the High Court does not have to hear any case it does not want to hear, save, as stated in Article III, "in all Cases affecting Ambassadors, other public Ministers and Consuls, and those in which a State shall be Party, the supreme Court shall have original Jurisdiction," the Court's so-called original jurisdiction.

The appellate jurisdiction of the High Court includes cases and controversies arising out of the state courts, military courts, regulatory commissions, so-called legislative courts, and, of course, lower federal courts. It is unclear whether Congress, under the language of Article III, "under such exceptions . . . as Congress shall make," can withdraw from the purview of the Court subject matter, but as it stands now, Congress has not excised any subject matter from the appellate jurisdiction of the Court. The rules for appeals, for procedure, and for evidence are all spelled out as well in *The Federal Rules of Civil Procedure*, the *Federal Rules of Appellate Procedure*, and *The Federal Rules of Evidence*. These rules, created by expert commissions of judges, lawyers, and law professors in the twentieth century, are themselves constantly reviewed and revised.

The relative burdens judges face in the federal and state courts are reflected in their dockets, or case loads. In the early part of the twenty-first century the Supreme Court took on about 70 cases a year. In 2002, the thirteen U.S. circuit courts of appeal handled a little over 52,000 cases. The 94 district courts heard about 272,000 cases that year. Special courts, for example, bankruptcy courts, handle many more cases. In 2008, for example, the federal bankruptcy courts groaned under 1.1 million filings.[31]

Even this cursory review of the structure and function of the state and federal judiciary reveals that the system of courts is parallel and hierarchical, but not uniform, orderly, and cohesive. Suitors can choose their venues and sometimes even pick their judges. This is called "shopping." Federal and state courts sometimes contend with one another. For example, in *Smith v. Oregon* (1990), a suit that went to the Oregon Supreme Court and the U.S. Supreme Court twice, the state court found that the First Amendment Free Exercise of religion clause barred the state unemployment office from denying benefits to an Indian who smoked peyote in a religious ceremony. The High Court remanded the case back to the Oregon Supreme Court, when the attorney general of Oregon appealed it, to hear arguments on whether the state's drug laws might bar certain kinds of drug use, even when part of a religious ceremony. The state supreme court reaffirmed its earlier decision and the state legislature changed the state's drug laws to allow the use of peyote during American Indian Church ceremonies. But the High Court, rehearing the case, overturned the decision of the state court. The U.S. Congress then passed the Religious Freedom Restoration Act of 1993, in effect chastising the High Court for its interpretation of the First Amendment Free Exercise of Religion Clause. President William Jefferson Clinton signed the bill into law. But the High Court overturned the act in *City of Boerne v. Flores* (1997). The Court made clear to the Congress that it was the final arbiter of the meaning of the First Amendment. One can only conclude from this awkward farrago that the adversarial system extended to the branches of the federal government.[32]

The nature and function of the courts reflect in part the difficulties of adjudicating cases in the nation of laws. Today most judges are highly trained and experienced lawyers before they become judges. They have grown up with the adversarial system and understand in a profound way that cases have more than one side to them. They are not automata administering inflexible codes, but common law judges applying precedent they select and statutes they interpret to a wide variety of fact situations.

Many judges admit that their judgments may be "value-laden," a reflection of their personal or internal moral standards and values, but in general they are "pretty cagey" about how far those values penetrate their judgments. The judge's moral views and the temper of his or her times certainly intrude into hard cases, cases that have no clear precedent or rule to follow. Judge Robert Keeton, perhaps the foremost modern student of American judging, has argued that judges' professionalism precludes decisions based solely on moral or social values. "Professionals are representatives of interests other than their own. They have professional responsibilities. They occupy defined roles." In their role as a judge, confronted with a case whose outcome is morally repugnant, "the judge usually concludes that the contribution one may make as a judge, committed to professionalism in judging, outweighs personal discomfort and leads to the choice to reach a result offensive to the judge's personal sense of justice."[33]

But Keeton's easy answer does not capture the agony judges face when moral scruple and settled law confront one another. Poignant examples of professionalism warring with personal ethos occurred in slavery cases like *Prigg v. Pennsylvania* (1842). Justice Joseph Story was a professional from head to toe, a law professor at Harvard as well as a respected member of the High Court and the author of treatises on the constitution and other legal subjects. He abhorred the institution of slavery and said so in his private correspondence. He nevertheless recognized slavery's constitutional posture—that the Rendition Clause dictated "No person held to service or labor in one state under the laws thereof, escaping into another, shall in consequence of any law or regulation therein, be discharged from such service or labor; but shall be delivered up, on claim of the party to whom such service or labor may be due." Story felt obliged by his professional duty as a judge to opine that the state of Pennsylvania could not try a slave catcher for kidnaping an alleged runaway. "Few questions which have ever come before this Court involve more delicate and important considerations; and few upon which the public at large may be presumed to feel a more profound and pervading interest. We have accordingly given them our most deliberate examination; and it has become my duty to state the result to which we have arrived, and the reasoning by which it is supported." As he wrote to a friend, shortly after the decision was announced and Massachusetts antislavery voices rose to condemn him: "You know full well that I have ever been opposed to slavery. But I take my standard of duty as a judge from the Constitution."[34]

Story's friends in the abolitionist community had tried to sway his vote in *Prigg*. Then as now the most powerful external influences on judges and judging are political. Many local or magistrates courts, including traffic courts and surrogates courts, and most state superior court and appeals court judges today are either appointed by elected officials (and then run for reelection—the so-called Missouri Plan) or run for election themselves. The intervals of these elections vary from state to state. Some states have mandatory retirement ages. Some of the elections are "partisan" and candidates declare their political allegiances. In other states, elections are nonpartisan and candidates face a yes/no vote. The supreme court bench of Hawai'i is appointive and may be reappointed for successive ten-year terms until the justice reaches the age of seventy. All federal judges are appointed by the president with the advice and consent of the Senate, an alternative to election intended by the framers to take the courts out of politics, but increasingly contentious confirmation hearings in the 1970s and after have made plain that the entire process of nomination, hearings, and confirmation are closely tied to political allegiances. After all, the Court is part of a political system, not some Olympian pantheon of juristic gods. As Henry J. Abraham, the foremost student of the nominating process, has written, "There is, of course, nothing wrong in a president's attempt to staff the Court with jurists who read the Constitution his way. All presidents have tried to pack the Court, to mold it in their images"—nothing wrong in that, so long as the justices are qualified in all other respects.[35]

Even if the judge does not see herself as a political figure, controversial decisions in highly charged political situations will always be read in political terms. The judge who does not at least admit this is only fooling herself. Some judges do have an explicit political agenda, and their decisions conform to this agenda. These may be liberal or conservative, pro-government or suspicious of government, Democratic or Republican. It was thus possible for observers of *Bush v. Gore* (2000) to predict how the justices of the High Court would vote on the disputed Florida presidential election.

True, protestations of fidelity to doctrine or concern for professional reputation may obscure such primary political commitments. The so-called "four horsemen" on the Taft and Hughes Courts, Willis Van Devanter, Pierce Butler, James McReynolds, and George Sutherland, all conservative Republicans, announced that "the universe was governed by inexorable laws, certain rights were inalienable; the Constitution was an unchanging document; the judiciary was a refuge against the excesses of the populace." On this basis they struck down, or tried to strike down, liberal New Deal legislation. Other judges, liberals in their politics, described the law as a flexible fabric to be tailored according to the needs of the moment. Jerome Frank, on the Second Circuit Court of Appeals in the 1940s and 1950s, believed that "judicial decision-making was rooted in subjective preferences," a realistic pose which "led him to argue that judges should have freedom and power to function as creative lawmakers. . . . So long as he understood the role of value preferences in judicial decision-making, he could interpret his function as one of enlightening the public as to the importance of certain social values." Arguing that the intent of the framers of the law is paramount ("originalism") lays a doctrinal foundation for conservative inclinations. After all, the founders lived in a time before women could vote and racial minorities had civil rights, and the law they framed permitted slavery. Others judges apply a modern sense of priorities to each case coming to their court. Some judges believe in restraint, leaving to legislators the task of making new law. Others believe in an activist judiciary, going beyond deference to the elected branches of government. Every judge will "lean" a little in the direction of his political beliefs, even if the bias is "subliminal."[36]

For the fact of the matter, and perhaps the most important fact the history of the American judiciary documents, is that from its inception to the present, appointment and tenure on the bench are highly political. The crown named to the bench those colonists who were deemed trustworthy servants of the empire and removed judges whose decisions did not square with the crown's desires. Though the tie with England and empire was entirely severed by the Revolution, judges in the new states and later in the federal courts were still politically connected. The first members of the newly created U.S. Supreme Court in 1789 were all reliable Federalists. President George Washington only nominated those men whose temper he knew and trusted. Over time, presidents have almost always named to the High Court members of their own political party, and political allies to the chief justiceship. Even the greatest of the chief justices, like John Marshall, Salmon P. Chase, Charles Evans Hughes, and Earl Warren, had political careers of their own before they went on the court. William Henry Taft had served one term as president of the United States. Some of the most influential of the justices, like Stephen J. Field and William O. Douglas, campaigned for president while they sat on the bench.[37]

It is not so obviously so, but certainly arguable, that in noteworthy cases some members of the High Court were looking at the election returns. The black robes they wear do not insulate the justices against shifts in public opinion, the triumph of one party or the other at the polls, or emerging consensus around new policy goals. The acceptance of New Deal initiatives like Social Security and the retreat from *Roe v. Wade* (1973) may have other explanations, but one cannot discount the impact of shifting national politics on the nation's highest court.[38]

The cases of two judges, one perhaps the most famous and certainly the most revered in the American judicial tradition, and the other largely unknown today but certainly deserving of our respect and attention, illustrate how judges dealt with politics and how politics dealt with judges. Virginian John Marshall would serve for thirty-four years as chief justice of the U.S. Supreme Court and leave a permanent impression on American constitutional law. Marshall was a politician at first, a Federalist who served in Congress and a secretary of state in one of the most tumultuous periods of American political partisanship. But during the entirety of his thirty-four years as chief justice, Marshall denied that he brought to the court a political agenda. He wrote opinions as if the law itself spoke. He was merely its oracle, applying the principles inherent in the Constitution to the great issues of the day. These issues might arise in a political form, but Marshall held that the Court was not a political institution in the same fashion as the other branches of the federal government.

On the Court, the pose was an effective one. Despite the clear political consequences of many of his decisions, he brought together members of the High Court from both parties, convincing them to join his opinions. In the process, he established the supremacy of the Court in matters of constitutional interpretation. He added to his Court's toolkit "judicial review," the authority to determine whether acts of Congress and state legislation were constitutional.

But from the time that John Adams nominated Marshall for the High Court center seat, in 1801, until his death in 1835, he was vilified by his political enemies among the Jeffersonian Republicans. One episode reflected this animus clearly. In 1804, with both houses of Congress firmly in the Republican camp, President Jefferson called on his party managers in the lower house to impeach the Federalists on the High Court. His first target was district court judge Timothy Pickering, whose bouts of insanity had become notorious. The Senate removed him after a short trial. Next was Associate Justice Samuel Chase, whose intemperately partisan remarks to jurors and counsel during sessions of the circuit court brought politics into the courtroom. Chase was impeached, and stood trial in the Senate.

Marshall knew that if Chase were convicted by the Senate, he would be the next target. During the opening days of the Senate trial of Chase, in February 1805, Marshall watched from the gallery. He saw Chase, broad shouldered and defiant but already terminally ill, writhing as fifty-two witnesses testified to his high-handedness in court, his badgering of Republican lawyers, and his acerbic grand jury addresses. Chase's counsel, Luther Martin, labored mightily to show that the prosecution witnesses were themselves Republican partisans. He also produced witnesses who denied that Chase had mistreated anyone in his court. Called to testify, Marshall was visibly ill at ease. One observer thought the chief justice plainly frightened. He conceded some points, and dodged others. He was not entirely friendly to Chase, but he did not provide the ammunition that the managers hoped would sink Chase. A Republican congressman complained that Marshall "discovered too much caution—too much fear—too much cunning" in his testimony.

Aid came from an unexpected quarter. Aaron Burr, the outgoing vice president and thus the president of the Senate, himself in disgrace for having mortally wounded Alexander Hamilton in a duel, questioned Marshall in a friendly manner, allowing him to qualify his answers to Chase's benefit. Chase was narrowly acquitted (none of the articles of impeachment obtained a two-thirds vote), and Jefferson's impeachment campaign came to an end. To his dying day, Jefferson regarded Marshall as a partisan in robes. Marshall never forgot the sting of Jefferson's vitriol.[39]

The great political issue of the early nineteenth century was slavery. Marshall was never a fan of slavery, though he owned a few slaves and did not free them at his death. He never directly challenged the South's "peculiar institution" and tried to avoid cases involving slavery. Marshall knew that a direct confrontation between the sections over the issue of slavery might lead to the dismemberment of the Union. John Belton O'Neall (1793–1863), the chief justice of South Carolina's Court of Appeals, was surrounded by slavery and could not dodge the issue. South Carolina's slaves outnumbered its free persons. What is more, his state would lead the South out of the Union in December 1860. O'Neall's judicial career was marred by politics of slavery and secession.

A child of Quakers who became a leader of the state's Baptists, O'Neall did not like slavery. He believed that slaves had the same souls as white folks and were the creatures of the same God. He was also a strong believer in the rule of law, and South Carolina law on slavery was harsh—introducing into his life and thought another of the law's apparently irreducible contradictions. Sitting in the state assembly, O'Neall helped pass a 1821law making the murder of slaves a felony. He believed that it raised the status of the slave from chattel (personal property) to "human being." He also favored allowing the testimony of slaves against white defendants in such cases, for the alternative was "an invitation to perjury." He failed in this effort.

The statute law of South Carolina, reflecting a consensus of the voters, fixed the slave in permanent bondage. O'Neall did not agree with the strictures of the slave code. In case after case involving slaves freed by wills but claimed as assets by creditors of the estate, O'Neall was faced with a conflict between his conscience and his duty. He believed that "the law, as we find it, and not as we would have it, is to be our guide." But O'Neall found ways to fulfill the wishes of testators and free their slaves.

Despite his opinions on slavery, O'Neall was much respected in the state. He led its temperance movement and promoted higher education for its young people. In addition to his long service as chief justice, he was named a major general in its militia. But during the presidential campaign of 1860, when many in South Carolina eagerly prepared for secession, O'Neall held out for the Union. In an editorial for the *Newberry (S.C.) Rising Sun*, he wrote: "We are, I fear, in evil times, rashness is in the ascendency. . . . How religious men can counsel violence . . . or array section against section is to me passing strange. . . . I have looked proudly to the stars and stripes and said 'these are the emblems of my free and happy home. Are these to be pulled down and trampled in the dust by mad and corrupt politicians?'" After Lincoln won, O'Neall continued to plead for calm and the Union, but when he begged for patience and fidelity to the Union on the steps of his own courthouse, hotheads pelted the chief justice with eggs and turnips. O'Neall remained the chief justice, a quiet witness to the exertions of war. He died in 1863, saddened by the economic devastation secession brought to his beloved state, knowing that law could not temper and the best of judges could not surmount the passions that politics stoked.[40]

One could multiply these stories endlessly. The barefaced

spite with which Louis Brandeis's opponents attacked him during his nomination hearings for the High Court in 1916; the gleeful mugging of Justice Abe Fortas by his critics when President Johnson nominated him to replace Earl Warren as Chief Justice in 1968; the attempted impeachment of William O. Douglas by his conservative critics in the Senate in 1970—all are proof, if more proof were needed, that judging and judges have never been separate from the politics of the nation.[41]

The result of this conflation of politics and judging, however complex, even subliminal or unconscious, is that the law in the court takes on the contest of the politics outside of the court. The greater the stakes in the case, the more invested by politics in the issues before the court, the more impact the court's decision will have on the politics of the time. And insofar as that politics is itself contested (for politics in a democracy always beckons competition), so the nation of laws bears that burden as well.

## Legal Educators

No one is more aware of the impact of forces outside the Court on its jurisprudence than legal scholars. One might not think of legal academics as a source of law, but in their service on legal commissions, in institutes, and in the law schools they have had nearly as great an impact as the formal institutions of lawmaking. From 1923, the American Law Institute, largely composed of legal academics after its founding by William Draper Lewis, dean of the University of Pennsylvania Law School, has produced Restatements of the Law that greatly influenced judges. The law professors on the Uniform Commercial Code project in the 1940s, led by Columbia University law professor Karl Llewellyn, reshaped the law of sales. The Model Penal Code of the 1950s was largely the work of law professors, notably Herbert Wechsler of Columbia, and it reformed criminal law in many states. The leading law schools' law review articles are cited in U.S. Supreme Court opinions.

No segment of academe grew faster in the twentieth century than the law schools. In 1910, Harvard Law School boasted nine professors and five lecturers. In 2007, its faculty included 149 men and women: chaired professors, visitors, clinical instructors, and fellows. Harvard is the largest law school in the country, but even the smaller schools rarely have fewer than twenty faculty.[42] Rodell whimsically reported how lawyers learned their arcane trade in the law schools:

> Law students . . . come to law school a normally intelligent, normally curious, normally receptive group. Day in and day out they are subjected to the legal lingo of judges, textbook writers, professors—those learned in the Law. . . . And once they have learned to talk the jargon, once they have forgotten their recent insistence on matter-of-factness, once they have begun to glory in their own agility at the mental hocus-pocus that had befuddled a short while ago, then they have become, in the most important sense, lawyers.

The picture is a little overdrawn but charming. For taking first-year law courses is not quite like learning the basics of a foreign language; it is more like learning to speak a foreign language idiomatically. Certain "terms of art" have meanings specific to their legal application. Even more important, the law teacher's repeated command to students to "think like a lawyer" begins to transform the way students read and argue the law. Looking for the legally justiciable issues in a fact situation, weighing points on all sides of a question, knowing what is a winning argument and what is puffery distinguish the able law student from one who might be happier in another profession.[43]

For a nation so obsessed with litigation and so prolific in its passage of laws, creation of courts, and breeding of lawyers, the standards for law practice and the means of legal education in the early years of the republic were surprisingly meager. There were no Inns of Court regulating the training of barristers, as there were in England. No one wishing to practice law had to have a law degree or even a college degree. Although Harvard Law School was established in 1817, and formal legal schooling was also available at the College of William and Mary and the University of Maryland, most lawyers "read law" in an established lawyer's office until they took the state bar examination. The books there were dog-eared volumes of old English classics like William Blackstone's *Commentaries on the Laws of England* (1765–1769), manuals of practice (with copies of various kinds of legal forms), multivolume editions of the state's appeals court opinions, and perhaps a law dictionary or "abridgment" (an encyclopedia of sorts) of English cases. The student also hand copied court papers and correspondence. It was an apprenticeship in a craft, completed when the student passed an oral examination by the state bar association.[44]

Recognizably modern legal education began after the Civil War. The number of law schools by 1900 exceeded 100. The number of students rose to the thousands. Night schools competed with the elite, university-based schools, the former catering to immigrants and minority students, the latter to university graduates. The American Bar Association demanded that law schools be accredited. Twenty-five of the leading law schools answered this call in 1900 by forming the Association of American Law Schools. Law schools could join the AALS if they offered the requisite number of courses, had the appropriate facilities, and their faculty was sufficiently well trained. The AALS and the ABA campaigned relentlessly against the night schools. The AALS also wanted law students to have a college education. These efforts created a two-tiered system, with some law schools offering what contemporaries regarded as prestige degrees. Such degrees made it easier for the student to find a good job, clerk for a judge, or enter the teaching profession. Today there are over 1,200 accredited law schools in America, and over 10,000 law professors.

A second prong of post–Civil War legal education was the shift in law school faculty members from part-time judges and practitioners (who still serve as adjunct instructors in almost all law schools) to a core faculty of full-time legal educators and scholars. Professors of law were to have no allegiance to a particular client's perspective. They were to be intellectually free to explore and argue the rules of law as they saw fit. As members of a university community they were also encouraged to interact with other faculty. Finally, as academics, freed from court-imposed deadlines, client meetings, and other practical chores, they were to have more time to simply think about the law, its problems, and its place in American society. From these professional law teachers would come powerful critiques and defenses of legal education, the laws, and the legal profession—though not at first, not until the twentieth century.

The first of the full-time professors was Christopher Columbus Langdell, dean of Harvard Law school from 1870 to 1895. He introduced the Socratic method of classroom instruction, later made famous by the movie *The Paper Chase* and the book *One L*. He insisted that his faculty be full-time teacher/scholars. Langdell instituted admissions requirements, added a third year of instruction, and published the first set of casebooks, following a precedent that John Norton Pomeroy of New York University Law School had set four years earlier.

Langdell's first casebook was a collection of old English cases in contracts that had, Langdell thought, an inherent logic. The abstract concepts of contracts, torts, and other discrete subjects in law had already emerged. Langdell and those who followed him believed that the cases were tied together by basic principles and students in law classes, like the students of the ancient Greek philosopher Socrates, could rediscover those principles through a scripted conversation with the instructor. "If these doctrines," Langdell wrote at the outset of his casebook, "could be so classified and arranged that each should be found in its proper place," as they were in his casebook, the hidden singing reason of the law would impress itself on the student. Langdell's method was so rigorous and comprehensive that numbers of students dropped out of the school and critics denounced him, but by the beginning of the new century most prestigious schools were adopting his Socratic methods and the pedagogy behind them.[45]

But no law school and no legal pedagogy was proof against the insistent, pervasive dictates of change. Ironically, the uniformity, clarity, and above all, the moral claims that Langdell made for law were challenged by the very full-time teachers that Harvard Law School and its peer institutions recruited. Publishing in another of Langdell's innovations, student-edited law reviews, these younger law professors like Roscoe Pound insisted that law was not a hard science, like physics, but a social science, like sociology. It must be understood in its time and place, as a product of human aspiration and party self-interest.

Over the nearly century and a half since Langdell introduced his program for a scientific, objective curriculum, the law professors have raised and raided camps of formalism and realism, neoformalism and neutral principles, critical legal studies and law and economics. The contracts course that was the linchpin of Langdell's jurisprudence rose and fell with these tides, for the law professors never marched in lockstep. In fact, at the best law schools the very reverse was true. Law professors were eager and persistent adversaries. Perhaps the Socratic method they used in their first-year classes rubbed off on them out of the classroom. Perhaps the very attraction of legal academe was disputatiousness. Whatever the origin, the law professors bashed one another all the time.[46]

Ordinarily, the bashing was polite, collegial, and professional though sometimes the language became a little more spirited. Thus Walter Wheeler Cook of Yale Law School called Harvard Law Professor Joseph Henry Beale's draft of a restatement of conflict of laws "grossly inadequate," antiquated, and just plain wrong. Jerome Frank mocked "Bealism" and coined the phrase "Bealy-mouthed." Beale, a gentleman, returned the insults with the mild reply that he could be "dogmatic" at times. He also ignored Cook's and Frank's suggestions. In the 1930s, when Dean Roscoe Pound of Harvard criticized the New Deal, his colleague Felix Frankfurter, a New Deal supporter, became apoplectic. Pound had hired Frankfurter, but Pound's "cowardice" and "scurvy tricks" demolished any gratitude the younger man might have had.[47]

Pound deserved better. He had dominated the jurisprudence of the first three decades of the twentieth century. He taught at and then led Harvard Law School until 1936. He believed that law and social policy had an essential relationship and became a leading spokesman for law in the public arena. But when he came face to face with practical contradictions deeply embedded in the modern law school he found that his ideology and his institutional commitments could not be reconciled.

Roscoe Pound never finished his law school education at Harvard, but this former Lincoln, Nebraska, botanist was not satisfied with reading law in his hometown and practicing law. He became a professor at the University of Nebraska School of Law, then its dean, then taught at Northwestern, Chicago, and from 1910 until his retirement, at Harvard Law School. He served as Harvard's dean from 1916 to 1936 and until his death in 1964 occupied the capacious front office at the law school's Langdell Hall.

Pound promoted a "sociological jurisprudence." Reading deeply in continental legal theory and influenced by sociologists,

Pound concluded that law was a product of various interests struggling to use law to their own ends. If law was to make society better, it must recognize and manage those interests. This privileged the legislative process, responsive to changing popular needs and interests, over a judicial branch mired in older ideas of jurisprudence. He called on law teachers to look for and expound on the real-life, real-time political, economic, and social processes that fashioned law. For himself, he wanted law to move away from the absolute protection of private property and consider the larger needs of society, including those at the bottom of the socioeconomic scale. A liberal Republican in the days when Republicans like Theodore Roosevelt demanded reform of politics, he promoted legislative reforms in the workplace and Progressivism in politics. He has been called a "Progressive pragmatist" for this reason.[48]

But as dean of Harvard Law School, the largest in the country and the most wealthy, Pound could not avoid the conflicts of interest about which he wrote. Much of the school's wealth came from the gifts of alumni, and the most generous givers were often the best-established members of the bar. They frowned upon liberal legal scholarship and liberal legal causes. The most galvanizing and polarizing of these causes in the 1920s, and the episode that demonstrated the limitations of Pound's liberalism, was the trial and conviction of two immigrant Italian political radicals, Nicola Sacco and Bartolomeo Vanzetti.

Sacco and Vanzetti were part of an anarchist group with ties all over Europe and in the Italian immigrant communities of New England. It was a time of anarchist violence, including bombings, and in response the notorious Red Scare, with its warrantless arrests of thousands of radicals of all kinds. For the alleged shooting of a guard and a paymaster in South Braintree, Massachusetts, on April 15, 1920, both men were arrested, tried, convicted, and sentenced to death.

During the Red Scare, Pound had spoken out against the

roundup of political dissidents without evidence of any crime, but he hesitated to join the public defense of the cobbler and the fishmonger. He was raising funds for a chair in criminal law and was a member of the Wickersham Commission investigating the effectiveness of federal law enforcement. For him to take sides in the Sacco and Vanzetti case would jeopardize his status and the reputation of his law school. Pound told Walter Lippmann that he thought the two defendants innocent, but when Lippmann asked Pound's colleague and fellow reformer Felix Frankfurter to approach Pound to speak out about his concerns, Frankfurter could not persuade Pound. On May 11, 1927, Frankfurter expressed his exasperation to Dean Charles Clark of Yale: "Opinions don't matter much until they are put to the test—until we hold them against resistance"—a not so oblique criticism of Pound. A P.S. excoriated "the shamelessness of trustees and alumni on this matter."[49]

Throughout the spring and summer of 1927, newspapers printed heated public exchanges over the case. Legal academics conducted their own discourse. When legal appeals had run out, and Pound's voice might still have tipped the scales in favor of a new trial, he refused to speak. He urged others to continue the protests, but as he had "a strong dislike of discussing cases while they are pending in court," he would not allow his private views to become public. Other academics were not so cautious. Clark wrote to Frankfurter on April 27, 1927, "We expect to send a protest signed by most of the members of the faculty, although as might be expected, some of the declinations seem surprising. I have written an article for the Yale Daily News, and shall probably speak at a student gathering this week." Clark understood what was at stake for the academics, as he wrote to Harrison Sheldon, a lawyer in local practice,

> We law teachers assume to be critics of the law. I take it that assumption is now well known and fairly generally

recognized. It seems to me that we should be wanting in candor and in courage, as well as in honesty to ourselves if we were willing to assume this role only as to commercial cases and backed down in cases of vitally more importance. I therefore felt in justice to my own profession and my idea of it that I was under the obligation to speak if the case demanded it.[50]

Not all the academics sided with Frankfurter and Clark. John Henry Wigmore, an expert on evidence at Northwestern Law School, thought the conduct of the trial by Judge Webster Thayer was perfectly reasonable. On April 25, he wrote an article for the *Boston Evening Standard* decrying the crime as "cold blooded" and the law professors' campaign for a new trial an "agitation." Clark privately fumed: "On that score I have found no lawyer ready to defend the trial . . . except the specious and misleading remarks of Dean Wigmore, who, as is well-known, was one of the unfortunate casualties of the [First World] war," a reference to Wigmore's part in the Red Scare. Sacco and Vanzetti were electrocuted on August 23, 1927, their guilt still a matter of controversy.[51]

Like Pound in the 1910s and 1920s, the next generation of legal academics became mentors of new generations of law professors. As Karl Llewellyn, one of these gifted teachers wrote in 1931, "Ferment is abroad in the law." In the law schools, "irreverent, iconoclastic, and steeped in the political tradition of Progressivism . . . young and energetic scholars" like Clark at Yale attracted a critical core of "legal realists," including William O. Douglas and Llewellyn. They in turn inculcated in the next generation of students, hence of future lawyers, judges, government officials, and teachers, a wariness of abstraction and formalisms and an embrace of the law as an instrument of reform. They brought to the classroom a passion for making the law a more useful tool for everyone, for law reform in its best sense. In its turn, legal realism gave way to philosophies of so-called neutral principles, then law and society, followed by critical legal studies and critical race theory, no pedagogical novelty ever totally sweeping the field of its predecessors, but each reinvigorating academic debate over the nature and purposes of law. What was true of Clark was true of the best of educators, a "care, concern, and patience in carrying his work to a conclusion."[52]

The Clarks and their ilk set a high standard for the modern legal educator. Poised in the classroom, concerned with law's effect on everyday life, modern legal teachers in the Pound-Frankfurter-Douglas mold are public intellectuals. The law professor has become a common sight on the American intellectual landscape, a talking head on cable news opinion programs. Some, like Harvard Law School's Laurence Tribe and the University of Michigan's Catharine Mackinnon, argued major cases before the Supreme Court and played a vital role in law reform.

Increased visibility has subjected the legal academy to increased scrutiny. The law professor is no longer (perhaps never was) safe in the ivory tower. That does not bother the great ones, as the whole nation becomes their classroom. But some law professors overstep the bounds, intermixing the zealous advocacy we expect of our lawyers with the deliberative neutrality and consistency we expect of our pedagogues. While writing articles defending the torture of suspected terrorists or the use of military forces to arrest suspects on American soil may or may not be acceptable in academe, its ethics is far more questionable when an academic working in the Department of Justice writes memos supporting these steps because he is told to do so (or thinks that his boss would appreciate it). Appointment to government office does not allow a legal educator to simply follow orders or to write what a superior wants to hear. We hold our legal pedagogues to a higher standard.[53]

Adversaries and partisans would seem to be the least likely people to promote the stability, adaptability, and progress of the law. But in our system, that is exactly what happens. The adversarial nature of our laws allows many voices to participate in the making and the execution of law. Partisanship brings politics into the law, but insofar as democratic politics itself derives from law, so law thrives on partisan viewpoints. Participation at all levels and access points to law means accepting and manipulating conflicting legal doctrines.

What is the value of mass participation with its attendant contest to the people who participate in legal activities? Adversarial process and partisan input affords some chance of success to everyone, which a uniform and unvarying law would foreclose. Improvement in the law is more likely to come from this broad participation than from the narrowed access that uniformity would allow. But there are times when a galvanized public and worried politicians put almost unbearable stress on legal process. Examples of these occasions are trials that test the very commitment to fairness in a nation of laws.

## 4

## *Criminal Trials*

There are more trials for serious criminal activity in the United States today than in any other western European nation. Indictment statistics over the past 200 years suggest that this is not a new phenomenon. If the criminal trial is in some sense a proof of the failure of a legal system (famous lawyer Robert S. Bennett once quipped, "If you have to go to trial, you have already lost"), why does a nation so committed to its legal regime countenance so many trials? Perhaps the multiplicity of criminal laws and the duplication of legal jurisdictions actually increases the number of trials, or at least criminalizes acts that in other nations are not offenses. Or perhaps criminal trial in America serves other, more complex social functions than bringing the accused to justice?[1]

It is for this latter reason that certain kinds of criminal trials fascinate lay observers and professional commentators. These trials are what Karl Llewellyn and E. Adamson Hoebel in their study of Native American forms of adjudication, *The Cheyenne Way* (1941), called "cases of trouble." The trials at the end of such cases challenge the norms of a society and tax the legal system to find just solutions to vexing questions. They stretch the imaginations and the wills of the parties and the lawgivers. I have selected four types of such trials. The first allowed society to define or redefine itself at critical moments. The second were highly publicized events so closely watched and so important to observers that their outcome changed the course of political history. The third posed tests of rights and privileges that affected large segments of society. The fourth type are so rich in expressions of fundamental ideas that these cases directed the subsequent course of the law. A nation of laws tests itself in such trials.[2]

In these cases, the trial was the closing stage of a law case the state waged against an individual or group of individuals. The state's intervention foreclosed the older alternative of blood feud and insured that crimes will not go unpunished. In the colonial era, most people accused of crime were punished in some way, usually with corporal punishment or fines, the primary purpose of criminal justice being order keeping. Today, the number of criminal prosecutions that result in trial varies from jurisdiction to jurisdiction, but rarely rises above 5 percent. The vast majority are "plea bargained" out of the system. The colonial trial itself was often no more than an argument in front of a judge and jury. There was little to prevent rumor and hearsay in testimony, and juries were free to make law as well as find verdicts of fact. In the early nineteenth century, judges and legislatures curbed jury discretion by introducing rules of evidence (what was admissible and what was not) and by taking from juries their power to determine points of law. Today, the prime objective is that innocent defendants not be punished for a crime they did not commit. Thus the aphorism that it is better that a hundred criminals go free rather than one innocent person be wrongly convicted. But that was not the case in Salem, Massachusetts, in 1692.[3]

## Societies under Siege: The Salem Witchcraft Trials

There were occasions in the past when some part or place in American society found itself under siege. Authorities feared that basic values were imperiled and deviance within the society undermined its harmony. The ties that held the community together frayed. At these times, a trial could determine who belonged and who did not belong in that community, who fit in and whose ways were unacceptably threatening. The trial would then enable the society to restate its values or redefine itself.

But such trials by their nature also reveal great rents in the fabric of law. For in late seventeenth-century Massachusetts one set of laws defined belonging in a community according to full church membership. Never easy to gain (it required a recital of fitness before the entire congregation) or to retain (for puritan society required congregants to observe and report on their neighbor's good conduct), it nevertheless created a visible church whose members recognized one another's piety. But another form of belonging lay entirely in the civil realm. It was bounded by criminal laws passed by the assembly and monitored by magistrates.

The witchcraft crisis of 1692 in Salem pit these two sets of laws against one another. An ugly combination of political uncertainty, widespread panic, and deeply held superstition led to a legal horror story. In the early winter, all of northern New England reeled beneath King William's war, a pitiless English-French war of raids and atrocities. Into the port city of Salem came boatloads of refugees from the frontier telling of almost unspeakable Indian horrors and devilish Roman Catholic priests. A settled politics at home might have quelled the panic, but Massachusetts was temporarily without a charter of government, awaiting the pleasure of the new rulers of England, William and Mary.

The tangled web of mistrust and animosity reached out to a rural village in the western corner of the township of Salem. Some in the village wanted to retain the services of Minister Samuel Parris. Others wanted him and his family gone. Quarrels over the retention of ministers were common in New England towns, but this one was carried on with great venom because it overlay a struggle between two powerful families, one supporting Parris, the other undermining him.

To all of these tumults was added the inexplicable illness of Parris's daughter. It was the little ice age, and the damp cold seeped into all of Salem Village's houses. Everyone was sick, and soon other girls in the village complained of the same symptoms as little Betsy Parris. Adults were baffled and fearful until the girls accused three local women, one of them Parris's slave Tituba, of being witches.

The men and women of early modern New England believed that the Devil could give to women and men supernatural powers, the power to travel in spectral form and harm the Devil's enemies. The prodding of parents and ministers refocused what might have been a combination of preadolescent anxiety and play-acting into accusations of a capital crime. Frightened by the hideous shapes of their own imaginings, the parents and preachers turned to the magistrates to scourge the witches and their satanic master from the land. One of these was Rebecca Nurse, a grandmother in her seventies, and a respected full member of the Salem Village church.[4]

The pretrial hearing of Nurse on March 24, 1692, was typical of the authorities' approach to the accusations. She had no legal counsel, and no one spoke for her, though her neighbors were all there. Her minister, Parris, took notes. She could only protest her innocence in religious terms. She could not prove it, because the civil authorities permitted her accusers to introduce spectral evidence. "Are you an innocent person relating to this Witchcraft?" Magistrate John Hathorne asked her, in front of a bevy of her accusers. Before Nurse could answer, Thomas Putman's wife cried out, "Did you not bring the Black man with you, did you not bid me tempt God & die? How often have you eaten and drunk [with] your own demon?" Hathorne pressed

Nurse: "What do you say to them?" Nurse pled, "Oh Lord help me" and spread out her hands in supplication, at which point Parris's notes indicated that "the afflicted were grievously vexed." Hathorne: "Do you not see what a solemn condition these are in? When your hands are loose the persons are afflicted."

Then the girls whose accusations began the crisis joined in, realizing that Nurse's religious protestations had no impact on the civil proceeding. "Mary Walcott (who often heretofore said she had seen her, but never could say or did say that she either bit or pinched her, or hurt her) & also Elizabeth Hubbard under the like circumstances both openly accused her of hurting them." Hathorne's mind was already made up: "Do not you see these afflicted persons, and hear them accuse you?" The evidentiary question was whether the accusers were indeed afflicted, but he assumed that to be so, and what he wanted from Nurse was a confession. But Nurse's plaintive piety came out as sinister stubbornness. "The Lord knows I have not hurt them: I am an innocent person."[5]

In May 1692, newly appointed Governor William Phips returned from England to find the jails overflowing with suspected witches. The colonial assembly had the power to create regular courts under the new charter, but it was not yet in session and something had to be done. Faced with the crisis, he used his discretion to fashion a special court. William Stoughton, the lieutenant governor, was the chief judge, and he determined to root out the witches. That meant once again allowing spectral evidence that only the alleged victims could see. The girls' demonstrations of spectral assaults at trial doomed the defendants, despite their pleas of long-established piety. Trial juries browbeaten by Stoughton and moved by the performance of the girls convicted all the defendants. By the end of the proceedings that spring and summer, fifteen women including Nurse and four men were hanged for witchcraft, and one old man, Giles Corey, was pressed to death with heavy stones for refusing to accede to the authority of the court. Nearly 200 more suspects were in jail awaiting their turn at trial. Four of the suspects had died in jail and many more were sick.

The leading ministers (except for Cotton Mather, who approved the conduct of the trials) protested against the proceedings and convinced minister Increase Mather, Cotton's father, to turn their criticism into a tract on the dangers of believing spectral evidence. He argued for the priority of the religious laws over the civil ordinances. Spectral visitations might be the Devil's instrument to fool the credulous and cast blame on the innocent. Permitting spectral evidence in court was playing the Devil's game. Increase Mather's work was widely circulated. Phips was convinced and ordered a stop to the trials. They would reconvene in the winter, but this time spectral evidence was not allowed. All but three women were acquitted at this new round of trials, and Phips pardoned them.

Witchcraft accusations recurred, but never again did a colonial court take them seriously. The whole of the trials, both the summer trials of 1962 and the winter cases of 1693, fostered a public crisis, a terrible time of soul searching and conversation among lawgivers and ministers. The result was a decision to drive spectral evidence from the courtroom. At a terrible cost, the trials enabled civil authorities to examine the impact superstition had in the courtroom and resolve to deny it a place. True, the invisible world in which specters lived retained its fascination in the popular mind. Ghosts and goblins are still a mainstay of popular culture. Periodically an avid prosecutor, an easily tutored victim, and a gullible jury will rush to judgment. If the times are ripe for panic, if outside enemies seem to have inside help, then the witch hunt will resume. The accused may be former Communists, student radicals, civil rights agitators, or suspected terrorists. A new set of trials will then test American values and determine who belongs and who must be scourged. A conflicted law whose outcomes cannot be reconciled with a deeper, democratic sense of justice will have the chance to examine itself.

## Turning Points: The Trial of John Brown

Trials can reveal—even themselves constitute—turning points in American history. When the divisiveness in existing law or a bitter rivalry among conceptions of law reflect critical divisions in the polity or society, a trial may quicken or redirect political events. No trial is a better example of this process than the trial of John Brown. When Brown attempted to raise a slave rebellion by occupying the federal arsenal at Harpers Ferry in 1859, the division between North and South, a division between free and slave states, became unbridgeable. Laws that had held together the fraying edges of union began to snap.

Slavery was the most divisive political question at the federal constitutional convention of 1787. The founders sought a compromise between freedom and free labor, on the one hand, and slavery and slave labor on the other. The federal Constitution never mentioned slavery but provided for a portion of the total of slaves to count in states' apportionment, allowed the despised international slave trade to continue until 1808, and most controversially, provided for the rendition of those owing labor in one state who fled to be forcibly returned to the state from which they came. Slavery was to be legal where state law established it and illegal when state law barred it. That arrangement was maintained by strong emotional and economic ties of nationalism and by a two-party system that stretched across the North and South. When tests of that compromise came to Congress or the federal courts, compromises were found—though the debates over these arrangements had become more and more acerbic in the 1850s.

By the eve of the presidential election of 1860, the legal

compromises designed to hold the union together had become occasions for dire warnings of disunion. Antislavery advocates in Congress decried a southern plot to expand an empire of slavery. Southerners in Congress threatened that any attempt to interfere with slavery would result in secession. Congress seemed deadlocked over the issue of expansion of slavery to the unorganized western territories, and efforts by presidents Franklin K. Pierce and James Buchanan to resolve the issue of Kansas' admission to the union as a slave state had only brought more controversy. When the Supreme Court, in *Dred Scott v. Sanford* (1857), found that slaves returned to slave states remained slaves despite residence in free states, there was a storm of protest in the North, but the decision did not lead to violent resistance—at least not until October 16, 1859, when Brown, his sons, and a group of twenty-one recruits seized the federal arsenal at Harpers Ferry, Virginia, and proclaimed their intention to lead a revolt of the slaves.

Brown was a galvanizing figure, either beloved or hated. In the Kansas Territory he had freed slaves, but he also bushwhacked pro-slavery settlers. With his interpretation of the Bible as his inspiration, he saw himself on a divine mission to uphold the higher law of freedom and equality. Some abolitionists in the North shared that vision, but his supporters in the North did not understand how frightening Brown and his ideas were to the South. On October 18, 1859, after a short siege, a wounded Brown and four of his followers were captured in a barn in Harpers Ferry. He had refused to escape when he could, during the early stages of the raid, and refused to surrender when faced with overwhelming federal force (led by Colonel Robert E. Lee). To some, he seemed principled; to others, insane. But the events had drawn the attention of the nation to the issue of slavery.

Brown and four of his men were held in custody in Charles Town, now a part of West Virginia, and charged in state court with treason against Virginia, inciting slaves to rebellion, and murder. Brown, unmoved by the charges, retorted that he obeyed a higher judge in a higher court. "If you want my blood, you can have it any moment, without this mockery of a trial." The trial began on October 26 and continued for a week. A grand jury found true bills on all three counts. Brown pled not guilty. The prosecution thought it had an easy case as well as a popular cause. Though his lawyers wanted Brown to plead not guilty by reason of insanity, Brown refused. "If I am insane, of course, I should know [it] more than all the rest of the world. But I do not think so." All that Brown's counsel could allege was that Brown acted on principle—but that principle, freedom for the slaves, was the very basis of the charges.[6]

The state's counsel explained why the outcome of the trial was so important to the South. Brown had "come into the bosom of the Commonwealth with the deadly purpose of applying the torch to our buildings and shedding the blood of our citizens." Brown was a revolutionary, and such conduct in Virginia, whatever its role in the American Revolution, and however much white Virginians lionized the heroes of that revolution, was no longer permissible. Brown "wanted the citizens of Virginia calmly to hold arms [i.e., do nothing] and let him usurp the government, manumit our slaves, confiscate the property of slaveholders, and without drawing a trigger or shedding blood, permit him to take possession of the Commonwealth and make it another Haiti." The Haitian slave revolt was apparently still fresh in Virginia memory. "For when you put pikes in the hands of slaves and have their masters captive" as Brown planned, the only result could be civil war.

The jury took forty-five minutes to find Brown guilty. Sentenced to death on November 2, 1859, Brown then gave a short speech meant not for the judge or jury, but for northerners who had followed the trial with intense interest:

In the first place, I deny everything but what I have all
along admitted, of a design on my part to free slaves. I
intended certainly to have made a clean thing of that
matter, as I did last winter when I went into Missouri, and
there took slaves without the snapping of a gun on either
side, moving them through the country, and finally leaving
them in Canada. I designed to have done the same thing
again on a larger scale. That was all I intended to do. I
never did intend murder or treason, or the destruction of
property, or to excite or incite the slaves to rebellion, or to
make insurrection. . . . This Court acknowledges, too, as I
suppose, the validity of the law of God. I see a book
kissed, which I suppose to be the Bible, or at least the New
Testament, which teaches me that all things whatsoever I
would that men should do to me, I should do even so to
them. It teaches me further to remember them that are in
bonds as bound with them. I endeavored to act up to that
instruction. . . . Now, if it is deemed necessary that I should
forfeit my life for the furtherance of the ends of justice, and
mingle my blood farther with the blood of my children
and with the blood of millions in this slave country whose
rights are disregarded by wicked, cruel, and unjust
enactments, I say let it be done.

Brown's martyrdom, or so antislavery advocates called it,
brought the Civil War closer. He had laid the legal division bare
in a way that the congressional debates and divided opinion of
the High Court did not. In the later forums, the debate turned on
the interpretation of the Constitution. Brown regarded the Constitution as a pact with the Devil. The only law that mattered was
the law of God, and that bade him and all who opposed slavery
use force. While northerners made Brown into a hero, southerners feared that his vision of blood would come to pass.

With all its fears of a northern-led slave insurrection aroused, southerners responded to Abraham Lincoln's victory in the 1860 presidential contest with anger and fear. On December 24, 1860, representatives to a secession convention in Charleston drafted and unanimously approved a "Declaration of the Immediate Causes Which Induce and Justify the Secession of South Carolina from the Federal Union." It was a legal document and in part it read: "The frequent violations of the Constitution of the United States, by the Federal Government, and its encroachments upon the reserved rights of the States, fully justified this State in . . . withdrawing from the Federal Union." Behind that constitutional theorizing was the apprehension that the North "have denounced as sinful the institution of slavery; they have permitted open establishment among them of societies, whose avowed object is to disturb the peace. . . . They have encouraged and assisted thousands of our slaves to leave their homes; and those who remain, have been incited by emissaries, books and pictures to servile insurrection."[7]

Brown's trial did resolve one issue. The slaves would not rise up against their masters. Wisely recognizing that resistance on the scale that Brown urged was futile, the slaves watched as white man's justice ran its course. No slave was tried for treason with Brown. No slave took up a pike that Brown's agents offered. When the war over slavery came, it was a white man's war because, in large measure, the divide over the nature of law was one that white men had created.

## Of Rights and Wrongs: The Trial of Susan B. Anthony

The Civil War settled the legal question of secession. The Union was to be perpetual. The Thirteenth Amendment, a wartime measure, settled the issue of slavery. Except for penal servitude, no one might be enslaved by another person. But when Congress drafted and the states ratified a series of civil rights acts and the Fourteenth and Fifteenth Amendments to clarify the legal status of the freed slaves, the language of these additions to the Constitution was far broader in implication. In particular, the Fourteenth Amendment was open ended: "No State shall make or enforce any law which shall abridge the privileges or immunities of citizens of the United States; nor shall any State deprive any person of life, liberty, or property, without due process of law; nor deny to any person within its jurisdiction the equal protection of the laws." The three clauses—privileges and immunities, due process, and equal protection—could be read to usher in a federally protected regime of rights. One of these, the right to vote, was protected against state obstacles in the Fifteenth Amendment.

Against the plain text of the latter two amendments lay another set of laws and legal attitudes—legal debilities of women. Common law denied to women full citizenship. They could not hold property in their own name if married, unless the state specifically permitted it. They could not vote without permission of the state. They could not hold office or enter certain professions without state waivers. Women, included in the Thirteenth and Fourteenth Amendments, were not specifically aided by the Fifteenth Amendment. Indeed, laws passed to prevent voter fraud in the Reconstruction South could be read to bar women from voting absent state permission.

On November 1, 1872, Susan B. Anthony, recently elected president of the National Women's Suffrage Association and a nationally known women's rights proponent, joined fourteen other women registering to vote in the upcoming presidential election. They announced that they had this right because all citizens had the right to vote. The nation watched as they exercised it. On Tuesday, November 5, 1872, four days after persuading the registrars to let Anthony and her compatriots register, they cast their votes in the First District of the Eighth Ward of Rochester, New York. As Anthony exulted in a hastily written note to her long-time friend and ally in the women's rights movement, Elizabeth Cady Stanton, "Well I have been & gone & done it!!"[8]

While many women across the country attempted to vote that presidential season, only Anthony's ballot inspired national headlines and raised the hopes of women in and out of the suffrage movement. The elation of Anthony and her allies did not last long. On November 14 U.S. Commissioner William Storrs issued warrants for the arrest of the fifteen women voters; four days later the federal deputy marshal arrested Anthony at her home in Rochester.

These events and the subsequent trial of Susan B. Anthony in June 1873 comprise one of the signal events in the history of the women's rights and the suffrage movement. Women's franchise, excluded from the text of the Fifteenth Amendment, brought to a head the frustrations of leaders and rank and file among the women reformers. Women had petitioned Congress to be included in the Fifteenth Amendment, to no avail. Anthony had violated a federal "enforcement act" of 1870 passed with the precise intention of criminalizing illegal voting in the South during Reconstruction—a remarkable irony given that the very women who so strongly supported the North in the Civil War, and joined with male abolitionists to support voting rights for black freedmen, were now to be punished under these acts.

The case came before the federal circuit court, over which presided newly appointed Supreme Court Justice Ward Hunt, a conservative New York Republican and no friend to women's rights (though he was a moderate supporter of the rights of former slaves). Hunt shortened the trial by directing the jury to find Anthony guilty.

Anthony had argued that women, as citizens, deserved all the rights of any other citizen. Hunt lectured the jury that

the right of voting, or the privilege of voting, is a right or privilege arising under the Constitution of the State, and not of the United States. The qualifications are different in the different States. Citizenship, age, sex, residence, are variously required in the different States, or may be so. If the right belongs to any particular person, it is because such person is entitled to it by the laws of the State where he offers to exercise it, and not because of citizenship of the United States.[9]

Hunt gratuitously hinted that he found the women's suffrage campaign ludicrous. "If the State of New York should provide that no person should vote until he had reached the age of 31 years, or after he had reached the age of 50, or that no person having gray hair, or who had not the use of all his limbs, should be entitled to vote, I do not see how it could be held to be a violation of any right derived or held under the Constitution of the United States."

Hunt instructed the jury that "the defendant is indicted under the act of Congress of 1870, for having voted for Representatives of Congress in November, 1872. Among other things, that Act makes it an offence for any person knowingly to vote for such Representatives without having a right to vote." The jury complied with the justice's instructions and found her guilty.

When Hunt asked Anthony if she had anything to say before he pronounced sentence, the following colloquy occurred, as much a signal moment in American legal history as John Brown's closing statement. Against Hunt's narrow construction of the statute, Anthony argued that constitutional rights—the penumbras of the Reconstruction Amendments—should be read broadly.

> Anthony—I have many things to say; for in your ordered verdict of guilty, you have trampled under foot every vital principle of our government. My natural rights, my civil rights, my political rights, my judicial rights, are

all alike ignored. Robbed of the fundamental privilege of citizenship, I am degraded from the status of a citizen to that of a subject; and not only myself individually, but all of my sex, are, by your honor's verdict, doomed to political subjection under this, so-called, form of government.

Judge Hunt—The Court cannot listen to a rehearsal of arguments the prisoner's counsel has already consumed three hours in presenting.

Anthony—May it please your honor, I am not arguing the question, but simply stating the reasons why sentence cannot, in justice, be pronounced against me. Your denial of my citizen's right to vote, is the denial of my right of consent as one of the governed, the denial of my right of representation as one of the taxed, the denial of my right to a trial by a jury of my peers as an offender against law, therefore, the denial of my sacred rights to life, liberty, property and . . .

Judge Hunt—The Court cannot allow the prisoner to go on.

Anthony—But your honor will not deny me this one and only poor privilege of protest against this high-handed outrage upon my citizen's rights. May it please the Court to remember that since the day of my arrest last November, this is the first time that either myself or any person of my disfranchised class has been allowed a word of defense before judge or jury . . .

Judge Hunt—The prisoner must sit down—the Court cannot allow it.

Hunt's peremptory instructions to the jury to find Anthony guilty became the subject of a congressional inquiry. He had fore-closed the chance for a genuine discourse, turning a trial into an inquisition. His action had unintended consequences. Shortly thereafter, judges would be forbidden from directing a verdict of guilty in a federal criminal trial. Anthony refused to pay the fine, and the authorities simply gave up trying to collect it. But Hunt's condescending and admonitory tone continued to echo in the halls of Congress and the language of the High Court. In its 1907 Citizenship Act, Congress declared that a woman born in the United States, hence a citizen under the Fourteenth Amendment, was still a second-class citizen. If she married a foreign national, she expatriated herself, losing the right to vote even where state law conferred it. If a male citizen of the United States married a foreign national, he did not lose his citizenship.[10]

In *MacKenzie v. Hare* (1915), Justice Joseph McKenna wrote for a unanimous U.S. Supreme Court affirming a California Supreme Court decision that a woman who married a British subject lost her right to register to vote. McKenna reasoned,

> The identity of husband and wife is an ancient principle of our jurisprudence. It was neither accidental nor arbitrary and worked in many instances for her protection. There has been, it is true, much relaxation of it but in its retention as in its origin it is determined by their intimate relation and unity of interests, and this relation and unity may make it of public concern in many instances to merge their identity, and give dominance to the husband.[11]

Fourteen years after Anthony died, the object of her transgression, female suffrage, would eventually come before a national referendum. The Nineteenth Amendment to the federal Constitution declared: "The right of the citizens of the United States to vote shall not be denied or abridged by the United States or by any State on account of sex." In 1922, Congress repealed the invidious distinction between male and female citizens who married foreigners—at the urging of female voters.

Women will not again lose the right to vote, but as Anthony

wrote near the end of her life to Elizabeth Cady Stanton: "Now this seems to me to be the false religion of this day. The old slaveocrats are bound to push out every man and woman of color from the *enjoyment of civil rights.* . . . On every hand *American civilization,* which we are introducing into Isles of the Atlantic and Pacific is putting its heel on the head of the Negro race." Anthony was prophet as well as pioneer. In the coming years, civil rights trials would focus on the rights of racial minorities. The same contest between discriminatory state and federal law on the one hand, and the equality the Reconstruction Amendments promised on the other, would mark these trials as it had marked Anthony's. Her argument would become the arguments of the Legal Defense Fund of the National Association for the Advancement of Colored People. Four generations later, Anthony's view of the law expressed at her trial would be fully vindicated.[12]

## Ideas in Court: The Trial of John Scopes

Anthony based her defense on her right as an American citizen to participate fully in the political process. Rights are not things— they are ideas, and some trials enable a test of competing ideas. These ideas need not be legal. They might reach deeply into the cultural and intellectual currents of the time. Law gives them a chance to parade in their finery, for the many parties at trial and those who observe the trial to decide what they think.

One such trial in 1925 revolved around two controversial sets of ideas—religious fundamentalism and the science of evolution. The prosecution of biology teacher John Scopes for telling his students about Darwin and evolution put Darwin, the Bible, and modernity on trial. The early 1920s saw in many parts of the United States, particularly in the South, a high tide of religious fundamentalism. Christian fundamentalists believe in the literal truth of the Bible, including the creation story. In 1924, Tennessee passed a statute making it a crime "to teach any theory that denies the story of divine creation as taught by the Bible and to teach instead that man was descended from a lower order of animals." Punishment was a fine.

The American Civil Liberties Union, founded in 1916 to help organized labor, had turned by the 1920s to free-speech cases. For the ACLU, the Tennessee law raised just such issues. Indeed, the case presented the first real opportunity to explore the concept of academic (teaching) freedom as a facet of free speech. During World War I, censorship and anti-German feeling combined to curb the free speech of teachers. Here, however, was an issue ready-made for academic freedom—science and freedom of thought versus the state.

Before World War I, scientific theories such as evolution were slowly making their way into high school biology textbooks. At the same time, mandatory high school education was becoming common throughout the nation, including the rural South. After the war, the supposedly godless science of evolution became a particular target of fundamentalist preachers and congregants, including such highly respected men as former secretary of state and Democratic presidential candidate William Jennings Bryan. Perhaps he hoped to regain lost celebrity status by leading the attack on evolution. Perhaps he was genuinely opposed to it. In any case, he made himself available to speak at every meeting he could against Darwin's ideas.

Dayton, Tennessee, was little more than a hamlet, but its leaders had a plan to bring the attention of the nation to the town. It began with a businessman named George Rappelyea. He convinced Scopes to admit that he had taught evolution to a class (as it happened, Scopes also believed that evolution was correct). The ACLU now had its client. They wanted former presidential candidate John W. Davis to represent Scopes, but

Clarence Darrow heard of the case and forcefully volunteered his services. Davis then declined to participate. The ACLU sent staff lawyer Arthur Garfield Hays to help Darrow, along with other counsel. The state was represented by two former state prosecutors and Bryan, who could not be held back.

Bryan and Darrow had known one another for nearly fifty years. Darrow had campaigned for Bryan's presidential bid in 1896. Now they were friendly adversaries. What began as a test case of freedom of speech and "academic freedom" was becoming a test case of science versus the Bible and modernity versus tradition, a trial over which the two giants of the law cast looming shadows.[13]

Although the outcome of the trial was obvious from its start on July 10, 1925—Scopes would be found guilty—the thousands in attendance, including many newspaper and radio columnists, were treated to a public airing of religious and scientific ideas. The prosecution's case was simple: call witnesses to prove that Scopes had taught evolution in the biology review class. Darrow and his cocounsel prepared to offer defense testimony from a cadre of scientists that evolution was good science and belonged in the biology curriculum. Correctly, the court ruled that this testimony was not relevant to the legal question of whether Scopes violated the law.

Stymied, Darrow asked if Bryan would take the stand and defend the Biblical version of creation. What followed was pure melodrama. (Indeed, it became the basis for the hit play and movie *Inherit the Wind.*) The trial moved from the overstuffed and brutally hot courtroom to the lawn outside. Darrow wanted to prove that a fundamentalist interpretation of the Bible creation story was bunk. Bryan wanted to show that the Bible could be taken literally. Five thousand spectators followed Darrow's and Bryan's Q-and-A on the literal truth of the Bible creation story:

Q (Darrow)—You claim that everything in the Bible should be literally interpreted?

A (Bryan)—I believe everything in the Bible should be accepted as it is given there: some of the Bible is given illustratively. For instance: "Ye are the salt of the earth." I would not insist that man was actually salt, or that he had flesh of salt, but it is used in the sense of salt as saving God's people.

Q—But when you read that Jonah swallowed the whale—or that the whale swallowed Jonah—excuse me please—how do you literally interpret that?

A—When I read that a big fish swallowed Jonah—it does not say whale. . . . That is my recollection of it. A big fish, and I believe it, and I believe in a God who can make a whale and can make a man and make both what He pleases.

Q—Now, you say, the big fish swallowed Jonah, and he there remained how long—three days—and then he spewed him upon the land. You believe that the big fish was made to swallow Jonah?

A—I am not prepared to say that; the Bible merely says it was done.

Q—You don't know whether it was the ordinary run of fish, or made for that purpose?

A—You may guess; you evolutionists guess . . .

Q—You are not prepared to say whether that fish was made especially to swallow a man or not?

A—The Bible doesn't say, so I am not prepared to say.

Q—But do you believe He made them—that He made such a fish and that it was big enough to swallow Jonah?

A—Yes, sir. Let me add: One miracle is just as easy to believe as another.[14]

Scopes was convicted, then the conviction was overturned on appeal (based on a technical error in the sentencing). Fifteen state legislatures had pending similar statutes to Tennessee's. Only Mississippi and Arkansas went on to pass these. They survived until the Supreme Court, in *Epperson v. Arkansas* (1968), determined that the Arkansas law violated the First Amendment ban on establishment of a religion. Arkansas had "tailored . . . teaching and learning . . . to the principles or prohibitions" of a "religious sect or dogma." But the debate between science and fundamentalism continues in new guises and finds its way into courtrooms as teachers or parents challenge evolution teaching or creationist teaching.[15]

Criminal trials that revealed sharp cleavages in social values; criminal trials that changed the course of history; criminal trials that tested competing conceptions of rights; and criminal trials that allowed a plain exposition of complex and controversial ideas demonstrated that the ambivalence and contest inherent in American law could provide a public forum for the airing of unpopular or controversial ideas.

Insofar as criminal trial illuminates the values underlying a nation of laws, it brings a special clarity to the atavistic struggle that is law. For in its infancy, the law of crime was a wager, a combat between individuals or groups. Law in American has never really left that vestige of the ancient agon behind. Trial forces advocates of one view or another to put up or shut up. But trial in the law has evolved as everything else in American law. Because the trial creates a text—transcript, news record, appeals court opinion—that can be revisited time and again, and seen with new eyes, unlike the ancient combat, the loser can become, in time, the winner, as a later, wiser age recognizes the folly or the malignity of an earlier period.

# 5

## *Critical Episodes*

As one can see in the four criminal trials of chapter 4, there are episodes in our nation's history when law seemed to fail to provide justice. Yet in many of these episodes, the people involved did not turn away from law. Instead, they turned toward it. Put in other terms, they thought the law vital even when it seemed the last resort. They could not do without it.

My thesis in this chapter is simple: we are a nation of laws that work because we expect law to perform vital functions for us at our most perilous moments. When we are in most need of solutions to critical problems, we turn to law. I have selected five of these episodes from American history, highlighting the part that law played. Though in all of them the law was stressed to the breaking point, in only one of them did it crack, and that episode is itself highly instructive. I have saved that episode for last, taking it out of chronological order, because it teaches us what happens when faith in law is lost.

To be perfectly candid, this chapter has a pedagogical subtext. Legal history courses are among the most exciting in the college curriculum, but legal history does not always find its way into other American history courses or into American history textbooks. The same subjects that appeared in earlier chapters of this book—the Salem witchcraft trials, for example—are there, but they are not treated as legal events. By refocusing our perspective in the episodes below, I want to show how legal history played a vital part in the larger American story.[1]

## The Stono Rebellion, South Carolina, 1739

The first and largest slave rebellion in the British North American colonies occurred along the Stono River in the South Carolina Low Country. The colony of South Carolina, a successful planter venture whose rice production made its landowners some of the richest men in the world, depended upon the labor of an enslaved black majority. Early in the morning of Sunday, September 9, 1739, near a bridge over the North Branch of the Stono River, a slave drain-digging crew killed two whites in a roadside store, spent the rest of the night and early morning marauding the countryside, and in the first light, bolted for freedom in Florida.

The people of the Stono region, black and white, watched as the slave band grew in numbers and boldness. The militia flew to arms. A confrontation between the militia and the slave band later in the day led to the killing of the ringleaders and the scattering of the remnant of the band. Slaves caught in the ensuing days' pursuit were summarily questioned and either forgiven or executed. The story is a tragic lesson in the horror of slavery, the simmering violence underlying race relations, the harshness of plantation regime in the colony, and the continuing influence of African warrior culture and Afro-Christian teachings in America.[2]

In what seemed to be an orgy of lawlessness, law actually played a central role. There were no formal trials, but the slaves were breaking the law. Armed insurrection, indeed any use of arms or violence against whites, was an offense punishable by death. The slave code specifically provided for freeholder courts—two justices of the peace and a body of planters—to hear and determine accusations of slave insurrection. The slave code including all this and much more was the most detailed and voluminous legislation on South Carolina's books. The militia, a legally constituted body one of whose tasks was insuring the security of the colony, was another major topic of colonial law. Slavery would have been impossible without the active participation of justices of the peace, judges, legislators, and all their works.

The slave code spoke to the white population more than the slaves. It required that all white males either participate in the nighttime patrols or serve in the militia. They were to carry guns to church and to town. They were to inspect slaves on the roads and on the waterways to check passes. But they did not. They hired slaves to fetch and carry, to cook and sew, and bought fish and fowl from slaves. Some even bartered liquor for the slaves' goods. Plainly, the law on the books did not match the law on the ground. It could not have—not if slave and free were to engage in the everyday social and economic interactions all societies require.

It was in these interstices of the black code that the revolt began. The law required that road commissioners supervise the slave work crews, but the summer was so hot, the savannahs surrounding the Stono River so mosquito ridden, and malaria so ubiquitous that no overseer stayed to see that the slaves returned to their home plantations. The revolt occurred because everyone involved violated the letter of the law, and that in turn because the law as written was simply not enforceable.

But after the revolt, a frightened and sober assembly turned once again to the law. Though it had failed, they still trusted it to control the black majority. In the revised code of 1740, slaves were not to carry weapons of any kind. Slaves were not to use musical instruments that might signal a rebellion. Slaves were not to carry on businesses of their own. "Be it enacted, that no owner, master or mistress of any slaves, after the passing of this act, shall permit or suffer any of his, her, or their slaves to go and work out of their respective houses or families, without a ticket in writing" from the owner. What may be even more important, the revised code was realistic about the relationships that must exist between whites and blacks. For example, if slaves acted for a master and had a pass, then the slaves might carry goods to market, sell and buy, offer their own skills in barter, even go about in boats and carts without supervision.[3]

On its face, even more repressive than older versions, the code of 1740 made compromises and concessions. The law supposed to make the slave stand in fear, the law that denied basic personhood to slaves, recognized—had to recognize—the humanity of the slave, because South Carolina society and economy could not be successful if the slaves and their masters did not cooperate. When the slave owners turned to law to embody their needs and their fears, slavery etched its ambiguities on the face of the law. These ambiguities created a human space between a harsh law and a sometimes lenient reality. Without some leeway to humanize slavery, the system itself could not function.

## The Seneca Falls Convention, New York, 1848

The next story is as far removed from the low tidal marshes of the South Carolina coast as one can travel—the "burned over" region of New York around Rochester, the site of the religious fervor of the Second Great Awakening, a hotbed of abolitionism, and the home of a remarkable group of women. We have already met one of them, Susan B. Anthony, whose mother, Lucy, took part in the event described below.

At Seneca Falls, midway between the cities of Rochester and

Syracuse, on July 19, 1848, a women's rights convention met, and over 300 people crowded the Seneca Falls chapel. In attendance were all manner of reformers, including advocates of abolition of slavery, world peace, and equal educational opportunities for women. Lucretia Mott's husband, John, officially chaired the meeting, but Lucretia and Elizabeth Cady Stanton ran the show.[4]

The problem was simply put and almost insuperable. Women's health and life expectancy were improving. A growing cadre of middle-class women were gaining a sense of themselves and their potential for improving the world around them. But that potential ran into legal impediments on every side. Women could not vote, hold office, enter many of the professions, or even, when married, own property in their own names except through exemptions. In some southern states laws allowed married women to own property separate from their husbands, but these statutes were thinly veiled attempts to shield the family from the husband's creditors.

The convention gained focus, urgency, and a program when Stanton, the daughter of a lawyer, presented a draft "Declaration of Sentiments." The declaration, modeled on the Declaration of Independence, listed the legal grievances of women.

> The history of mankind is a history of repeated injuries and usurpations on the part of man toward woman, having in direct object the establishment of an absolute tyranny over her. To prove this, let facts be submitted to a candid world. He has never permitted her to exercise her inalienable right to the elective franchise. He has compelled her to submit to laws, in the formation of which she had no voice. He has withheld from her rights which are given to the most ignorant and degraded men—both natives and foreigners. Having deprived her of this first right of a citizen, the elective franchise, thereby leaving her without

representation in the halls of legislation, he has oppressed her on all sides. He has made her, if married, in the eye of the law, civilly dead. He has taken from her all right in property, even to the wages she earns.

The declaration was the opening shot in a battle for legal equality for women that would rage for another seventy years, and in other forms still rages today.[5]

What was the cure for women's legal debilities? More law. Better law. Fairer law. The laws on the books reflected widespread male (and to a lesser extent female) assumptions about the weaker sex. After two days of debate over how fast to go toward women's equality, the gathering agreed unanimously on all but one of the proposals. The demand for voting rights passed with a slim majority. But as a legal manifesto and a program for the future, the declaration was a success.

If one accepts some version of the struggle-triumph-vindication version of the story of suffrage for women, one may miss the real message that the Declaration of Women's Rights bore. It was not that women were simply entitled to what men claimed as their own, but that women could be different from men, with different needs and aims, and yet these should not prevent women from enjoying equal legal treatment. It is this divided character of legal feminism, based simultaneously on equal treatment under the law and separate personhood, that ran all through the women's rights movement. "Each generation of women's activists leaves an unfinished agenda for the next generation. First Wave suffragists fought for women's citizenship . . . but left many customs and beliefs unchallenged." Among these were basic economic questions that law did not begin to address until the Civil Rights Act of 1964. The failure of the Equal Rights Amendment movement proves that in certain respects, "the struggle for women's human rights has just begun."[6]

But the point here is that failure did not deter women from

turning to law for redress. When political and social ills needed remedy, women saw in law an avenue for their advancement. Even when, as at Seneca Falls, women were not lawyers, law-makers, or judges, they trusted that some place could be found for women's rights in law.

## John C. Calhoun Speaks, Senate Chamber, Capitol, Washington, D.C., 1850

The next episode comes from the tense days of 1850 on Capitol Hill, as congressmen debated the admission of California as a free state and the proposal for a new fugitive slave law. California would tip the balance in the Senate in favor of free states— leaving the South with a minority in both houses of Congress. Southern state legislators brayed defiance and held a secession convention in Nashville. Southern members of Congress demanded concessions from their northern counterparts lest that convention lead to disunion. Senator John C. Calhoun of South Carolina dreaded the prospect of secession but knew it was a possibility. On March 4, a dying Calhoun lay in a chaise next to his desk as a colleague read the speech Calhoun had drafted. Calhoun's subject was the fugitive slave issue, and the new law that created federal commissioners to assist in the capture and return of runaways.[7]

Calhoun believed that although law seemed to provide an ever-diminishing space for the South's "peculiar institution," only in law could one find the safety the South demanded. Indeed, only in law reform could the Union survive.

> The equilibrium between the two sections in the government as it stood when the Constitution was ratified and the government put in action has been destroyed. At that time there was nearly a perfect equilibrium between

the two, which afforded ample means to each to protect itself against the aggression of the other; but, as it now stands, one section has the exclusive power of controlling the government, which leaves the other without any adequate means of protecting itself against its encroachment and oppression.

Without any legal means, that is. For Calhoun, law itself was at stake in the conflict between the sections: "Had this destruction been the operation of time without the interference of government, the South would have had no reason to complain; but such was not the fact. It was caused by the legislation of this government, which was appointed as the common agent of all and charged with the protection of the interests and security of all." Without the protection of friendly legislation, southern slave property lay open to northern pillage.

Calhoun told his colleagues that the remedy for political stalemate was new and better law:

What is to stop this agitation before the great and final object at which it aims—the abolition of slavery in the States—is consummated? Is it, then, not certain that if something is not done to arrest it, the South will be forced to choose between abolition and secession? . . . There is but one way by which it can be, and that is by adopting such measures as will satisfy the States belonging to the Southern section that they can remain in the Union consistently with their honor and their safety. There is, again, only one way by which this can be effected, and that is by removing the causes by which this belief has been produced.

The solution was the passage of laws—"measures"—that would guarantee to the southern slave holder his property: the Fugitive Slave Law of 1850. Calhoun wanted a legal solution to what

quite perspicaciously he saw as a legal problem. Law had created the problem—half a nation slave, half free. Law could mend
it. At least that is what the lawyers like Calhoun who led the
nation hoped.[8]

Behind the politics of the Fugitive Slave Law of 1850 was a
legal program of real sophistication, but a problematic program.
The bill was innovative, entailing the creation of an in-depth, discretionary federal bureaucracy, a network of commissioners with
powers to hear and determine cases of suspected runaways, at a
time when the federal government was small, poorly funded, ill
staffed, and antagonistic to large bureaucratic enterprises.

> That the commissioners above named shall have
> concurrent jurisdiction with the judges of the Circuit and
> District Courts of the United States, in their respective
> circuits and districts within the several States, and the
> judges of the Superior Courts of the Territories, severally
> and collectively, in term-time and vacation; shall grant
> certificates to such claimants, upon satisfactory proof
> being made, with authority to take and remove such
> fugitives from service or labor, under the restrictions
> herein contained, to the State or Territory from which
> such persons may have escaped or fled.

The fugitive slave commissioners' procedures were administrative—no due process, no jury, no confrontation or cross
examination, no counsel for the captured suspect.

> Whereupon the court shall cause a record to be made of
> the matters so proved, and also a general description of
> the person so escaping, with such convenient certainty as
> may be; and a transcript of such record, authenticated by
> the attestation of the clerk and of the seal of the said court,
> being produced in any other State, Territory, or district in

which the person so escaping may be found, and being
exhibited to any judge, commissioner, or other officer
authorized by the law of the United States to cause
persons escaping from service or labor to be delivered up,
shall be held and taken to be full and conclusive evidence
of the fact of escape, and that the service or labor of the ·
person escaping is due to the party in such record
mentioned. And upon the production by the said party of
other and further evidence if necessary, either oral or by
affidavit, in addition to what is contained in the said
record of the identity of the person escaping, he or she
shall be delivered up to the claimant.[9]

The contradiction between the provisions of the new law
the South wanted and earlier formulations of the limits of federal
power the South had championed was obvious. In its wake, the
Fugitive Slave law of 1850 created new and critical tests for law
enforcement and the law-abiding. Northern states' antislavery
advocates responded with so-called personal liberty laws. These
laws interposed themselves between the suspected fugitive slave
and the federal commissioners. The state laws mandated a rudi-
mentary due process—the production of evidence, the suspect's
chance to defend himself, and in some cases a jury trial. In effect,
the Personal Liberty laws nullified the Fugitive Slave law, putting
the northern states in the same posture that South Carolina
adopted in opposition to the tariffs of 1828 and 1832.

The new federal law and the responding state laws clashed.
Calhoun's hopes to use law to maintain two nations, one free
and one slave, were dashed. As Abraham Lincoln told his audience during the senatorial debates with Stephen Douglas, in
1858, the "house" that was so divided "could not stand." But Calhoun and his successors viewed the act differently. For them, it
was a proof that the federal government would honor its commitment to the right to private property of all its citizens. That

right was embodied in the Fifth Amendment to the federal Constitution: "No person shall be . . . deprived of life, liberty, or property, without due process of law . . . nor shall private property be taken for public use, without just compensation." In *Dred Scott*, Chief Justice Taney cited the amendment as support for the proposition that slaves might be taken anywhere in the land without the owner fearing that his property would be taken from him by federal law. Leading Georgia lawyer and scholar Thomas R. R. Cobb's *An Inquiry into the Law of Negro Slavery in the United States* (1858) agreed that "this review of the decisions of the courts of the Union, shows that the weight, both of numbers and authority, preponderate in sustaining those conclusions." The law was clear. "Upon the slave being subsequently found within a slaveholding State, the master's rights and authority were not impaired by the temporary sojourn of the slave within the limits of a non-slaveholding state."[10]

But *Dred Scott* no more settled the issue than the Fugitive Slave Act of 1850, and Cobb's treatise only demonstrated that the conflict between the law of freedom and the law of slavery had grown more pronounced as the decade came to a close. Still, in the face of all contrary indications from the politics of the time, Taney and Cobb, like Calhoun, all leading lawyers, assumed that law could put the national dispute over slavery to rest. One might dismiss their efforts as politically naive, but the fact remains that when all else seemed to point to the spread of discord, they relied on the law.

Even as they withdrew from the Union, elected members of southern state secession conventions couched their decision in legal terms. Then delegates from the seceding states came together to write a constitution for the Confederate States of America resembling to a remarkable degree the constitution of the nation they left behind. The failure of law had ripped the nation apart, but the lawyers still hoped law could knit its riven sections into a law-abiding whole.

## FDR Introduces the New Deal, Washington, D.C., 1933

The Great Depression of 1929–1941did not leave the million dead of the Civil War, but with millions out of work, thousands of banks gone bust, and the fearful specter of communism and fascism looming, it was a crisis of momentous consequences. Newly elected Democratic President Franklin D. Roosevelt's inaugural address, on March 4, 1933, was truly part of a critical episode in American history.

That address and the steps Roosevelt took in the following 100 days has rightly been regarded as a personal and a political triumph. It was also the beginning of an epochal shift in American public law. In the address, Roosevelt uttered the rallying cry, "The only thing we have to fear is fear itself," but the substance of the address was not just psychological or political or economic or moral. It was also legal. One forgets perhaps too easily that Roosevelt attended Columbia Law School, and though he did not finish, he did become a member of the New York State bar and he practiced law with a major New York City firm.[11]

Roosevelt told the nation, "Our greatest primary task is to put people to work. This is no unsolvable problem if we face it wisely and courageously. It can be accomplished in part by direct recruiting by the Government itself, treating the task as we would treat the emergency of a war, but at the same time, through this employment, accomplishing greatly needed projects to stimulate and reorganize the use of our natural resources."

Pursuing this goal, Roosevelt would ask Congress to pass laws empowering the executive branch to create job programs. "Hand in hand with this we must frankly recognize the overbalance of population in our industrial centers and, by engaging on a national scale in a redistribution, endeavor to provide a better use of the land for those best fitted for the land. The task can be helped by definite efforts to raise the values of agricultural products and with this the power to purchase the output of our cities." Administrative agencies would set prices, regulate production, and insure a fair return on labor. "It can be helped by preventing realistically the tragedy of the growing loss through foreclosure of our small homes and our farms. It can be helped by insistence that the Federal, State, and local governments act forthwith on the demand that their cost be drastically reduced." Mortgage moratoriums, assistance to banks, and direct subsidies were all legal programs. "It can be helped by national planning for and supervision of all forms of transportation and of communications and other utilities which have a definitely public character." There was even a hint of socialism in the notion of economic planning—but all under the constitutional regime of the founders.[12]

The New Deal legal program was a veritable stew of old and new. Some of its new agencies looked a lot like older Progressive Era administrative bodies. Other agencies, like the National Recovery Agency, had precedent in World War I emergency measures that turned the federal government into the full-fledged partner of banks, industries, farms, public works, education, technology, transportation, and labor. Perhaps its initiatives never fulfilled their aims. Perhaps the major achievement of Roosevelt's domestic policies was a return of confidence and pride. Some called these steps the salvation of capitalism. Others excoriated the New Deal for abandoning capitalism. A balanced assessment is that Roosevelt "did mend the evils of the Depression by reasoned experiment within the framework of the existing social system. He did prevent a naked confrontation between orthodoxy and revolution."[13]

Whatever else the New Deal was, it was also a testing time for American law. In its willingness to experiment with administrative rule making, its commitment to labor equality at the bargaining table, and its introduction of the welfare state safety net, it expanded the social and economic obligations of government to the people. Some scholars believe that the "New Deal constitution" shifted law from its older primary objective of the protection of private property to solicitude for individual welfare and dignity. Others find only differences of degree in the New Deal programs, linking them to older Progressive initiatives. But there is no doubt of the fact that Roosevelt and his Brains Trust saw in law the salvation of the nation.[14]


## Abraham Lincoln's First Inaugural Address, Washington, D.C., 1861

The last of the episodes in this chapter provides a lesson of what happens when Americans turned to the law and found it wanting. Lincoln's first inaugural address, a message to both sections of the country on March 4, 1861, could not have come at a more critical time for the nation. Seven states had already seceded from the Union and formed the Confederate States of America. Southern congressmen had made their farewell speeches with varying degrees of bluster and sadness and departed the capitol for their homes. The outgoing chief executive, James Buchanan, a Pennsylvania Democrat of southern sympathies, was left without a cabinet. All southerners, they too had left. The incoming Republican majority had pledged to deny slavery a place in any of the western territories, and compromise efforts, including the proposal for a constitutional amendment to allow slavery in the territories, had failed.

Lincoln, a consummate state politician, had little direct experience of the turmoil the federal government in Washington, D.C., had experienced over the past decade. His one term in the House of Representatives had not distinguished him as a national leader. As he rode east in a special railroad car, he prepared what would become a classic of oratory, famed for its conciliatory tone and its deep religious resonances. As a political effort, it gained high marks as well. For Lincoln's speech "was a blend of political cunning and bedrock idealism," the "points and counterpoints about slavery and the Constitution" a summary of two decades of debate.[15]

But Lincoln, like Calhoun, was a lawyer, and he thought like a lawyer. Indeed, his legal career, a very successful one in Springfield, absorbed far more of his time and effort than his political career. He hoped that a legal solution might be found to regain the trust of the slave South and convince its leaders to abandon secession. With the gift of hindsight one can see that this was a forlorn hope, but a lawyer arguing what may seem, in retrospect, a lost cause remains a zealous advocate. Lincoln framed his appeal in legal terms, as if in a closing address to a jury, in this case, a hostile one. "I have no purpose, directly or indirectly, to interfere with the institution of slavery in the States where it exists. I believe I have no lawful right to do so, and I have no inclination to do so."

Lincoln specifically addressed the fears that the John Brown case had raised.

> Resolved, That the maintenance inviolate of the rights of the States, and especially the right of each State to order and control its own domestic institutions according to its own judgment exclusively, is essential to that balance of power on which the perfection and endurance of our political fabric depend; and we denounce the lawless invasion by armed force of the soil of any State or Territory, no matter what pretext, as among the gravest of crimes.

Lincoln also answered the fears that Calhoun had noted in his speech to the Senate, a decade earlier, as though the two men faced one another in court, arguing a point of law.

> It is scarcely questioned that this provision was intended by those who made it for the reclaiming of what we call

fugitive slaves; and the intention of the lawgiver is the law.
All members of Congress swear their support to the whole
Constitution—to this provision as much as to any other.
To the proposition, then, that slaves whose cases come
within the terms of this clause "shall be delivered up" their
oaths are unanimous. Now, if they would make the effort
in good temper, could they not with nearly equal
unanimity frame and pass a law by means of which to
keep good that unanimous oath?

Secession raised a series of vital and vexing legal questions.
Under the federal Constitution, could states secede? Lincoln was
firm on this point, again basing his argument on a lawyer's reading of the Constitution.

I hold that in contemplation of universal law and of the
Constitution the Union of these States is perpetual.
Perpetuity is implied, if not expressed, in the fundamental
law of all national governments. It is safe to assert that no
government proper ever had a provision in its organic law
for its own termination. Continue to execute all the
express provisions of our National Constitution, and the
Union will endure forever, it being impossible to destroy it
except by some action not provided for in the instrument
itself.

To Lincoln, the conclusion was inescapable. "It follows from
these views that no State upon its own mere motion can lawfully
get out of the Union; that resolves and ordinances to that effect
are legally void, and that acts of violence within any State or
States against the authority of the United States are insurrec-
tionary or revolutionary, according to circumstances." Seen in
this light, as the summary argument of a lawyer before the
nation as jury, the final passage makes perfect sense.

I am loath to close. We are not enemies, but friends. We must not be enemies. Though passion may have strained it must not break our bonds of affection. The mystic chords of memory, stretching from every battlefield and patriot grave to every living heart and hearthstone all over this broad land, will yet swell the chorus of the Union, when again touched, as surely they will be, by the better angels of our nature.[16]

In what Eden might the better angels choose the life of the Union over its death? For Lincoln, the answer was law. If the southern leaders stepped back from the precipice of secession and joined with him in a legal search for a legal solution to their concerns, disunion could be averted. That is why he offered the olive branch of a constitutional amendment.

But what did Lincoln want from the seceding states' leaders when he said in his first inaugural address, "I am loath to close"? He had already begged,

Before entering upon so grave a matter as the destruction of our national fabric, with all its benefits, its memories, and its hopes, would it not be wise to ascertain precisely why we do it? Will you hazard so desperate a step while there is any possibility that any portion of the ills you fly from have no real existence? Will you, while the certain ills you fly to are greater than all the real ones you fly from, will you risk the commission of so fearful a mistake?

In effect, he pled for a larger and longer discussion of slavery in the Union. He offered no resistance to the passage of a constitutional amendment guaranteeing slavery where it existed because a national debate on such an amendment would expand and extend the conversation among sectional leaders. He asked the South not to act irreversibly or in haste. But his call fell on deaf ears and the Civil War came. No one wanted it, but the end of discourse left no one any other option.

In all of these critical episodes, law does not immediately come to mind, but in all of them, when Americans needed to resolve disputes, assert authority, call for reform, or plead for restoration of an older order they turned to law. The stresses and contentions in each of the episodes, part of the larger political and social context in which the parties turned to law, then imbedded themselves onto the legal solutions proposed. In a nation of laws, that is what one should expect—that in times of crisis Americans would turn to law; that law would bear the marks of crisis.

The trust in law did not always repay itself. In 1861, Lincoln asked for more time and space, for a longer period of reflection about how law might resolve the crisis. The confederate states were not disposed to allow that time; though individuals did suggest legal palliatives, these were brushed aside. Yet even if law did not enable Americans to resolve every major political, economic, and social contest, it provided a mechanism for expressing the contesting values and, for a time at least, managing the contesting interests. I call these "discursive spaces," and they are the subject of the closing chapter.

# 6

## *Discursive Spaces*

In 1885, Oliver Wendell Holmes Jr. called law a "magic mirror" of society and politics. Law did more than simply reflect the controversies of contemporary society and politics. It transformed those controversies. The nation of laws was continually reinventing itself. The means, in part, were what I call discursive spaces. At moments in our history, in those virtual places, Americans debated what law should and should not be. The result was a law constantly reexamining itself, responding to new currents in thought and new forces in society and politics, keeping the law fresh.[1]

These discursive spaces were occasions when the entire country watched and listened to the conversation over the shape and function of our laws. The constitutional convention of 1787, the passage of the Reconstruction Amendments from 1865 to 1870, and the debate over the constitutionality of the New Deal were such moments. Then, political crisis imprinted itself on law as political leaders looked to law to solve political problems. But a political crisis was not a necessary precursor to the opening up of such discursive spaces. They appeared whenever the controversy over a particular area of law or event in law caused adversaries to come together and converse while the nation listened.[2]

## *Oliver Wendell Holmes Jr. and Freedom of Speech*

Holmes played a major role in one of those conversations. During World War I, Congress passed an espionage act that punished with up to twenty years at hard labor in a federal prison any act or conspiracy to act to undermine the draft or the war effort. Under this act, radicals, pro-German speakers, and even pacifists were convicted in federal courts. Appealing to the Supreme Court, these speakers at first found no friend in Justice Holmes. A thoroughgoing realist, he had no illusions about the limitations of liberty in times of national peril. Upholding the conviction of a German Socialist who opposed the war, Holmes wrote for the Court that, "We admit that in many places and in ordinary times the defendants in saying all that was said in the [antidraft] circular would have been within their constitutional rights . . . [but] the character of every act depends upon the circumstances in which it is done. The most stringent protection of free speech would not protect a man in falsely shouting fire in a theater and causing a panic."[3]

The war over, President Woodrow Wilson dispatched American troops to help overthrow the Bolshevik revolution in Russia. In support of the revolution four Jewish immigrant radicals in New York City wrote a pamphlet in Yiddish and dropped copies of it on the streets of the Lower East Side. Part of it read, "Do not let the Government scare you with their wild punishment in prisons, hanging and shooting. We must not and will not betray the splendid fighters of Russia. Workers, up to fight." The High Court upheld their conviction under the wartime Espionage Act, using Holmes's formula. Holmes, however, joined by Justice Brandeis, dissented in *Abrams v. U.S.* (1919). He wrote, "Now nobody can suppose that the surreptitious publishing of a silly leaflet by an unknown man, without more, would present any immediate danger that its opinions would hinder the success of the government arms or have any appreciable tendency to do so."

But there was something far more precious at stake than the freedom of four silly radical immigrants.

> When men have realized that time has upset many fighting faiths, they may come to believe even more than they believe the very foundations of their own conduct that the ultimate good desired is better reached by free trade in ideas—that the best test of truth is the power of the thought to get itself accepted in the competition of the market, and that truth is the only ground upon which their wishes safely can be carried out. That at any rate is the theory of our Constitution. It is an experiment, as all life is an experiment. Every year if not every day Americans have to wager our salvation upon some prophecy based upon imperfect knowledge. While that experiment is part of our system I think that we should be eternally vigilant against attempts to check the expression of opinions that we loathe and believe to be fraught with death.[4]

Holmes denied that he had changed his mind. He suggested that the situation was different in *Abrams* from the situation in the earlier freedom of speech cases and that the former cases were rightly decided on their facts. But for anyone reading the opinions, and for the subsequent legal history of the First Amendment and freedom of political speech, there were no real differences among the cases. Instead, the contradiction between the application of the two formulas created a space in which theorists, jurists, philosophers, political observers, legislators, and judges could examine the meaning and the utility of free speech. Zechariah Chafee at Harvard Law School and Judge Learned Hand on the First Circuit Court of Appeals, along with Holmes's colleague on the Court, Louis Brandeis, suggested the changes in the clear and present danger rule in conversations with Holmes. Holmes heard their voices.[5]

Holmes's invocation of a free marketplace of ideas gave that discursive space a name. It was a marketplace. The metaphor was free enterprise, ironic in light of Holmes's own skepticism about free enterprise, but the metaphor's power was great. In time, it was the metaphor, not the majority decision upholding the conviction of the four radicals, that came to stand for free speech in America. Multiplicity and contention enabled an ongoing conversation about free speech that a single formula would not have allowed.

## FDR and the "Packing Plan"

Debates over the meaning of the Constitution provided many discursive spaces in which contending voices encouraged Americans to seek a deeper understanding of the law. From 1934 to 1936, in a series of body blows to the New Deal, a majority of the High Court struck down the National Recovery Administration and other federally imposed regulations of labor and commerce. President Roosevelt, who watched the Court with a wary eye, had as early as 1934 floated the idea of adding justices to counterbalance the conservative majority on the High Court bench. In 1937, after a smashing victory at the polls, Roosevelt announced a plan to revise the membership of the Court. Congress had done this before, adding justices or (at the end of the Civil War) reducing the number of justices. Roosevelt would have added justices to the court for every justice over the age of 70, in effect "packing it" with New Deal supporters. From the vantage point of their new building, dubbed "the marble palace" by journalists, all of the justices viewed the packing plan askance. No one knew what Roosevelt's plan would bring, or if Congress would accede to the president's wishes. In fact, the Senate quashed the initiative. The packing plan debate seemed on the surface another evidence of the conflicted character of American law, but the six months of debate created a discursive space to examine what New Deal innovations were constitutional, and what lay outside the pale.[6]

On March 9, 1937, Roosevelt told the nation that the Court had left its proper judicial moorings and become a "policy-making body." That function was presumably left to the elected branches of government, in this case the Presidency and the Congress. He framed the debate as one on the separation of powers in the Constitution. In effect, he was also arguing that the president was the final arbiter of the meaning of the Constitution. The Court could not reply directly, for the Constitution itself required that a "case or controversy" come before the Court. Roosevelt knew that the National Labor Relations Board provision of the Wagner Labor Relations Act was already on the Court docket, as was the Social Security program. The Court would soon have its case or controversy to respond to the president. But Chief Justice Charles Evans Hughes, like Roosevelt a former governor of New York and something of a politician himself, was already writing to the Senate Judiciary Committee, friends in academe, and the media opposing the plan. By the late spring, most newspapers had gone on record against the plan. Why?[7]

The debate over the plan in Congress and in the public arena revealed the huge reserve of legal capital the Court had banked. Venerated as an institution, the Court could draw upon this fund to resist Roosevelt's plan. But the controversy did not end with this stalemate. In the next two cases that the Court decided, a narrow majority upheld both the NLRB and the Social Security system. In the discursive space created by the conflicting views of law, the Court found that deference to legislative bodies in times of crisis was an acceptable constitutional pose.[8]

Senator Hugo Black, an Alabama Democrat, strongly supported the Roosevelt plan on the Senate floor. His results-oriented approach to earlier New Deal initiatives, and his disappointment with the Court, inclined him to this position. But the debate in the Senate spurred the largely self-educated Black to think more seriously about the Constitution and how to read its provisions. Black's participation led him toward a strict interpretation according to what he believed the framers meant. While his history was not always accurate, the impact of the debate on his thinking was profound. It was thus ironic that Roosevelt gleefully appointed Black, whose views on court packing had changed, to the Court's first vacancy in 1937.[9]

While Black was reading the framers, scholars like Harvard's Arthur Holcomb and Edward Corwin of Princeton, with the enthusiastic assistance of Charles Clark, dean of the Yale Law School, and Felix Frankfurter were providing intellectual ammunition for the packing plan. Their idea, a brilliant fusion of old and new concepts of the Court, was that a constitutional amendment was in order to limit the age of justices. The old idea was the notion that Congress (which initiated amendments) could change the number of justices. The novelty was an age limitation. In later years just such age limitations would appear in law for many occupations. The alternative preferred by the administration incorporated the age limitation and dispensed with the amendment. Although the packing plan failed, its penumbras spread out from Congress into the academic community and the media. The groundswell of opposition, in part orchestrated by the Republican Party, nevertheless reminded the president that the Court was a venerated institution, whatever the current disjoint between its views of his powers and his own views. As Joseph Rauh, then Justice Benjamin Cardozo's clerk, later recalled, the packing plan had a wonderful energizing effect on the thinking of everyone concerned. Some it "scared stiff," while others it caused to rethink conventional views of separation of powers.[10]

### Martin Luther King's Letter from the Birmingham Jail

The civil rights movement opened many discursive spaces. But the most remarkable of them came in the early 1960s. The civil rights marchers in the Deep South in the 1960s rejected the proposition that they must simply obey established law when it promoted racial injustice, and they disobeyed state and local ordinances repeatedly and openly. Led by Dr. Martin Luther King Jr. they practiced "civil disobedience," though not every civil rights leader agreed with a plan for massive protests.[11]

From the Birmingham City Jail, on April 16, 1963, when the entire campaign for legal equality hung in the balance, King wrote to other ministers who had doubts about his course:

> In any nonviolent campaign there are four basic steps: collection of the facts to determine whether injustices exist; negotiation; self purification; and direct action. We have gone through all these steps in Birmingham. There can be no gainsaying the fact that racial injustice engulfs this community. Birmingham is probably the most thoroughly segregated city in the United States. Its ugly record of brutality is widely known. Negroes have experienced grossly unjust treatment in the courts. There have been more unsolved bombings of Negro homes and churches in Birmingham than in any other city in the nation. These are the hard, brutal facts of the case. On the basis of these conditions, Negro leaders sought to negotiate with the city fathers. But the latter consistently refused to engage in good faith negotiation.

The only recourse seemed to King to be nonviolent direct action. But civil disobedience did not displace legality. The civil rights activists disobeyed unjust laws in order to compel recalcitrant white southern authorities to change the law. "My friends,

I must say to you that we have not made a single gain in civil rights without determined legal and nonviolent pressure. Lamentably, it is an historical fact that privileged groups seldom give up their privileges voluntarily." King realized that within the law were warring opposite impulses. The Legal Defense Fund of the NAACP had worried that direct action might "hinder" or roll back civil rights gains in the court. But a strategy of litigation alone, without civil rights leaders' willingness to march, to protest, to go to jail, would allow the injustice of Jim Crow to remain law. Without the willingness to face violence that bigoted police officials countenanced, a new legal regime would never be born.[12]

The civil rights movement created a discursive space in the law, allowing lawgivers in the South and in the nation's capital to rethink how segregation worked. In that discursive space, a space filled with arrests and marches, court cases and finally the Civil Rights Act of 1964, Americans confronted the national disgrace of segregation and the racism on which segregation rested. The civil rights movement is not over, but the legal rights of minorities are no longer in question.

## The *"Joint Opinion"* in Planned Parenthood v. Casey

The High Court's civil rights decisions represented a reversal of older precedent. In this, the respect the country gives to its High Court played a vital part in the general acceptance of its turnabout. Veneration for the Court and a powerful view of its function in American society marked another discursive space, this time within the Court's chambers. In 1973, the U.S. Supreme Court found that the right of privacy guaranteed by the Constitution applied to the decision to terminate a pregnancy. In *Roe v. Wade*, Justice Harry Blackmun, writing for a 7 to 2 majority, opined that the Fourteenth Amendment's Due Process Clause afforded grounds to invalidate state laws prohibiting or severely impeding a woman's right to seek medical assistance for an abortion. But privacy, however derived, did not grant the absolute right to abortion. States had a right that grew as the pregnancy continued, so that "at some point in time [in the pregnancy]" the state could assert a compelling interest in protecting the potential life of the fetus.

Neither Blackmun nor the majority of the Court for whom he wrote "was in a position to speculate" on the medical question of when life began, nor did the Court think that the states could turn religious or moral presumptions into medical facts, but his opinion offered a formula to answer the legal question of when the state could restrict abortions. During the first trimester, the state was not to intrude into the doctor-patient relationship. At some point during the next trimester, after "viability," the state might act to protect fetal life, even going so far as to ban abortion except to save the mother's life. The Texas and Georgia statutes challenged in *Roe* and its companion case, *Doe v. Bolton*, failed to measure up to this standard, and so were void.[13]

That landmark opinion stood out in an increasingly burned-over landscape of pro-choice and pro-life discourse. The abortion debate drew in the American Medical Association and a variety of doctors' groups seeking control over the patient-doctor relationship; the American Bar Association and the American Law Institute, siding with the pro-choice forces; and feminist organizations, regarding the right to an abortion as a woman's right to control her own body. On the other side were the hierarchy of the Roman Catholic Church, seeing life beginning at conception; a political coalition of newly active fundamentalist Protestant churches; and after 1980, the Republican Party. Various states responded in widely divergent ways to *Roe*. Some tried to impose crippling regulations on abortion by refusing to allow it in public hospitals, refusing to fund abortions with public monies, requiring long waiting periods and consent from parents and husbands, and even prefacing the regulations with religious statements about the sanctity of unborn life. Some anti-abortion groups sponsored protests at clinics providing abortion counseling and procedures. The perfect storm of political and cultural controversy had etched itself on the law, leaving a mael-strom of conflicting regulations and inconsistent legal opinions.[14]

While the storm of controversy over abortion law still rages, there were moments in its course of remarkable calm when a discursive space opened and the controversy itself provided the foundation for vigorous restatements of the function and author-ity of law. One such moment was the so-called joint opinion of Justices Sandra Day O'Connor, David Souter, and Anthony M. Kennedy in *Planned Parenthood of Eastern Pennsylvania v. Casey* (1992).

When news of the voiding of its 1982 anti-abortion statute reached the Pennsylvania state legislature, its majority reacted by passing another restrictive act. The governor, a pro-life Democrat named Robert Casey, helped draft a new law, which passed in 1988. It included provisions that the Supreme Court had nullified in earlier cases, including a twenty-four-hour wait-ing period and a scripted informed consent in which the doctor was to review all the alternatives to abortion for his patient and remind her that the state could gain child support from the father. The statute also provided for notification of parents (with a judicial bypass), the patient's written statement that she had notified or tried to notify her spouse, and the compiling of infor-mation on patients that could, under certain circumstances, become public. The statute was challenged by three abortion providers and counselors, including Planned Parenthood of East-ern Pennsylvania and a doctor who filed a class action suit on behalf of all doctors who performed abortions in the state.

*Planned Parenthood v. Casey* arrived at the Supreme Court in 1992 and, given the makeup of the High Court, seemed to be the case that Chief Justice Rehnquist and Justice Byron White (both of whom had dissented in *Roe*), joined now by Justices Antonin Scalia, Kennedy, and Souter (if not O'Connor), needed to reverse *Roe*. But that did not happen.

Without revealing their mutual effort to anyone else on the Court, Justices Kennedy, O'Connor, and Souter began to meet and soon determined to write a "joint opinion" upholding both *Roe* and the Pennsylvania statute, and in the process offering a thoughtful and powerful reading of the purpose of such compromises.

Kennedy opened the joint opinion with a recital of the history of the case with words that surprised everyone in the courtroom, delighting some and infuriating others. "A jurisprudence of doubt" pervaded the Court's rulings on abortion, but the authors of the joint opinion agreed "the essential holding of *Roe v. Wade* should be retained and once again reaffirmed." Kennedy read that holding to have three equally important parts. The first was the right to abort a fetus in the first trimester "without undue interference from the state." This formulation led naturally to the next principle, that the state had an interest in the potential life of the fetus from conception and so undid Blackmun's formula completely, only holding the state to a rational standard of regulation. It could not prohibit an abortion, but it could heavily regulate the conditions for abortions. The third principle was that after "fetal viability," the state could "restrict abortions," subject only to exceptions for the mother's life or health.[15]

Souter's portion on stare decisis followed. Its tone was less elevated and more straightforward than Kennedy's, as one might expect in a discourse on such a dry subject, but thoroughgoing meticulousness was already Souter's hallmark. When confronted with a call to overturn well-settled precedent, the Court must engage in "a series of prudential and pragmatic considerations." In particular, had related principles of law so changed or the world so altered that the old rule no longer had "significant application or justification"? He read *Roe* to limit state power rather than to establish a fundamental right, which, again as the chief justice later noted, was an odd reading of *Roe* at best and perhaps also disingenuous. But Souter knew that his take on the case differed from *Roe*'s author, and like Kennedy he reached outside the confines of the law books for his authority. "The inquiry into reliance counts the cost of a rule's repudiation as it would fall on those who have relied reasonably on the rule's continued application." An unwanted or forcible pregnancy was not like a contract dispute. "The ability of women to participate equally in the economic and social life of the Nation has been facilitated by their ability to control their reproductive lives." Insofar as the "Constitution serves human values," to undo *Roe* would be to betray the hopes and plans of millions of women.[16]

Justice O'Connor concluded the joint opinion with the reasons why the provisions of the Pennsylvania law (less the spousal notification requirement) passed muster under the undue burden test that replaced the trimester test in Blackmun's original opinion. Indeed, although her portion was the longest, it was the easiest to explain, for she had merely to recite, like a mantra, that "a finding of undue burden is a shorthand for the conclusion that a state regulation has the purpose or effect of placing a substantial burden in the path of a woman seeking an abortion of a non-viable fetus." In the rest of her portion she merely "refined" the analysis of the circuit court whose opinion she and the other joint authors, now joined by Rehnquist, Thomas, Scalia, and White, affirmed. O'Connor seemed particularly aware of matters of fact in her portion of the joint opinion. Some scholars suggest that the joint opinion reflected O'Connor's general approach to law and lawmaking on the Court as well as her particular view of *Roe*. Clearly the joint opinion expressed her strong commitment to the importance of the integrity of the Court as well as her belief that ordinary people must be able to rely on the Court when settled interests like privacy were at stake.[17]

Whether the concepts in the joint opinion stand the test of

time does not matter so much as the way in which they demonstrated how, in a discursive space, the confusion of the laws promoted a larger clarification of the value and purpose of law. If *Roe* fails in coming years, the occasion of that fall will undoubtedly accompany another discursive space and further refinement of what we want from our laws.

## After the O. J. Simpson Trial

Not every discursive space was filled with high intellection or involved basic constitutional principles. In the upscale Brentwood section of Los Angeles, California, on the evening of June 12, 1994, a "horrific yet routine domestic-violence homicide" became "a national drama, one that exposed deep fissures in American society." The "race card" played by counsel for the defense turned a straightforward question of circumstantial and scientific evidence into a test of a nation's nerves. The defendant was former professional football star and sometime movie actor O. J. Simpson. After a televised trial that pitted a famous defense team against two assistant district attorneys, the jury brought in a verdict of not guilty. In the course of the trial and the months of soul searching and book-contract signing afterward, another discursive space opened. The trial seemed a perfect mirror of the contradictions in a nation of laws. Was the apparatus of law enforcement so prejudiced that no police investigation could be trusted? Was the law that governed trial so misshapen that an obviously guilty man could beat the rap with the aid of high-priced lawyers? Had a racially biased jury found a verdict contrary to the evidence? Had a publicity-loving judge turned the trial into a circus and all the participants into clowns; or was the system itself broken—134 days in court being too long for any criminal trial?[18]

Whatever one concludes about the quality of justice for the

defendant or the two victims in the trial, the subsequent debate was immensely valuable insofar as it opened up the criminal justice system to public observation. In the discursive space that the post-trial debate created, two veteran litigators explored the meaning of the criminal law. One was Vincent Bugliosi; the other was Alan Dershowitz. Both were controversial figures in their own right—Bugliosi one of the most effective county prosecutors in the country and Dershowitz a successful criminal appeals lawyer. Both had achieved a measure of fame in the courtroom, Bugliosi for prosecuting Charles Manson and his "Family," Dershowitz for gaining a retrial of Claus von Bulow in the attempted murder of his wife. As a former L.A. prosecutor, Bugliosi thought that Simpson could have been convicted. Dershowitz, after months on the defense team, disagreed.

Bugliosi was outraged at the incompetence of all the members of the prosecutorial and defense teams, but his conclusion rested on legal history, not courtroom histrionics. "It is my firm belief that the not-guilty verdict in the Simpson case has historical origins, conscious or otherwise, in the maltreatment, most physical, of blacks by white police officers throughout the years." It was a verdict on history, not present fact. In fact, the police did not frame or conspire to frame Simpson, and despite some discrepancies in times and eyewitness testimony, did a fairly credible job gathering evidence. The District Attorney's office made the most egregious mistakes, in failing to present incriminating evidence and fumbling the opportunities it had. The judge as well allowed too much latitude to the defense. But all of these missteps were understandable in light of the situation in Los Angeles at the time. No one wanted more race riots, and L.A. had suffered more than its share.[19]

But Bugliosi was worried about a more pervasive problem. In an America whose cable television stations clamored for more coverage of the trial, the media gave the case "a disproportionate amount of publicity." What is due proportion may be in the eye of the beholder, but a trial waged in the fickle eyes of so many beholders (viewers by the millions followed the case on Trial TV) put immense pressure on the criminal justice system. While trials must be public and speedy, the nearly year-long media event violated the spirit of the Fourth Amendment.[20]

Finally, Bugliosi stated that he would not have agreed to defend Simpson had he been asked, because he thought Simpson guilty. By implication, he was saying that the Simpson defense team, including Dershowitz, surely knew that Simpson was guilty and agreed to defend him anyway. Everyone is entitled to a defense, but everyone cannot afford, as Simpson could, a blue-ribbon defense team. Bugliosi knew that the fate of any defendant depended as much on the quality of legal representation as the fact of innocence or guilt. In an adversarial system, how far can a lawyer go to represent a client? Bugliosi was certain that members of the Simpson defense team engaged "in a concerted, unprofessional, and unethical effort" to "deny the people their right to a fair trial."[21]

Dershowitz's defense of the defense was just as practical and detailed as Bugliosi's, but it did not matter to Dershowitz whether Simpson was guilty. What mattered was the fairness of the trial to the defendant and to all others similarly situated. Dershowitz is a brilliant lawyer and student of the law. He is also a fierce advocate for his position in whatever setting he might find himself. He knew that much legal opinion targeted the trial and the defense team for abusing the system, and so had a personal stake in the debate that Bugliosi lacked.

Dershowitz had his own list of problems with the trial, but the list only partially overlapped Bugliosi's. The "less than exemplary" conduct of all the legal people undermined public faith in the outcome of the trial. It took too long and the expert witnesses reveled in obscurity. The lawyers "placed their own agendas" before their sworn interests, and the judge was not always able. But the real problem was that a criminal trial was not "a quest for the truth," and should not be, as it was in colonial times, a demonstration of the authority of the government. The test of trial could and should not be collapsed into the verdict a jury rendered. It would be easy to convict defendants on a lower standard of proof, but the result would be that innocent people, in particular people the government wanted to put away, would disappear. Trial would become part of a regime of tyranny. When Dershowitz wrote these words, in 1995 and 1996, the detention of suspected terrorists was nearly a decade in the future, but his warning was prescient.[22]

An ear attuned to legal conversations in discursive spaces like this does not hear jarring voices of special pleaders. Instead, Bugliosi and Dershowitz had a common point. The criminal law does not adequately respond to police procedure at one end of the process or to jury nullification at the other end. A trial should bring these now discordant and contradictory legal actors into closer alignment. Police must not racially profile or abuse on the basis of race. Juries should not try to react to the general perception of racial discrimination by acquitting individuals against the clear pattern of facts.

Not every legal controversy opened discursive spaces. Sometimes the tumult following a legal event actually closed down discourse. Sometimes the discourse extended over decades, with no apparent resolution in sight. When competing sets of values or contending interests were unwilling to look for compromise, the discursive space was filled with shrill noise instead of reasoned conversation. But each discursive space allowed the law to refine and renew itself. Discursive spaces provided a nation of laws with creative insights and practical improvements.

## *Epilogue:*
## *The Future of a Nation of Laws*

The argument of this book is that we are a nation of laws, a complex and sometimes perplexing notion. American law is contested every day. But the contests are not dysfunctional. The controversies that law spawned created discursive spaces in which many Americans debated the value and future shape of legal precepts. Because these controversies were not ephemeral, because law was the place where important people turned to settle important disputes, the competition for favorable legal outcomes provided the intellectual and social impetus for experiment and reflection.

Competition and contest are the necessary concomitants of a system of laws with many access points. As James Madison wrote in Federalist No. 10 about factions and partisans, "As long as the reason of man continues fallible, and he is at liberty to exercise it, different opinions will be formed. . . . From the protection of different and unequal faculties of acquiring property, the possession of different degrees and kinds of property immediately results; and from the influence of these on the sentiments and views of the respective proprietors, ensues a division of the society into different interests and parties." The only way to control these divisions was in a nation committed to law. And as more and more diverse voices are able to join in the debate over how to make better law, the result has been a progress, albeit uneven progress, from legal exclusiveness to inclusiveness and from privilege for a few to dignity for all.[1]

We are and always have been a nation of laws. Those laws have guided the hands of those in power and will continue to do so. The law will retain its complex pattern as long as American society retains its own larger complexities. The law will continue to reflect these as Americans turn to it for aid and comfort. Contest and competition in the law will continue to generate those occasions of reflection and intellectual creativity, the discursive spaces that allow the law to realign itself to social and political realities. For in that ability to adjust to changing mores and values, the law becomes a living thing.

That is my faith. But what if I am wrong? What if the deeper harmonies I hear in the overlapping voices of legal contention are no more than cacophony on which I have imposed an arbitrary and self-satisfied order? If the discursive space collapses into a black hole of discord, the enterprise of doing law fails entirely. It happened in 1861. A civil war over abortion rights seems unlikely. A civil war over civil rights, feared by some, did not happen. But might the mechanisms that make us a nation of laws fail just when we need them most, when civil unrest becomes a critical threat to the legal system itself? The authorities' response to the civil rights and antiwar demonstrations of the 1960s was hardly reassuring, nor was the official lawlessness of the antiterror campaign post 9/11. A nation of laws is not proof against the indifference of those who have little faith in law.

But those who have faith in the law have a powerful ally in its history. As I finished this collection of essays, I happened on a signed, complimentary copy of Morris Dees's *A Lawyer's Journey*. It was a gift for my family's support of his Southern Poverty Law Center. Dees is a superb advocate and fierce adversary, but above all a man who believes that the law can serve social justice. On the last page of his deeply moving autobiography, he wrote that in the courtroom he aimed "to lift the jurors above the simple facts of the case and give them a chance to render a decision that will be part of our history of justice and fairness." As he knew from his own experience, that history has much to apologize for. But it also has the capacity to elevate our spirits and remind us of "what we believe in as a people and a nation."[2]

If law is the magic mirror of society and the glory of the United States is its diversity, then law in a nation of laws should match that diversity. If democracy thrives on managed and mannerly contention, law should embrace that contention. If democracy can only survive by finding the means to accommodate dissent, law should provide the means. Do we have a nation of laws? Yes. Are those laws for all? Not quite. But getting there. Are those laws perfect? No, and if the lesson of our legal history is precedent, there will be no closure. But if the argument of *Nation of Laws* is correct, it is better that the laws are in a state of becoming, rather than in being, for the ongoing discourse is as important as the product of the discourse.

# The Sources for American Legal History

I have been researching and writing American and English legal history since the early 1980s. In those years, a few classic works stood out in a largely undeveloped terrain. Since that time, legal history has become a fertile field worked by academic historians and academic legal scholars, practicing lawyers, political scientists, anthropologists, sociologists, journalists, and freelance authors. There is a remarkable collegiality among these students of our laws sometimes lacking in other fields of historical scholarship. The results of their labors are a cornucopia of books and articles.

The working historian's research and writing reflect the nature of her sources. These take two forms. Primary sources are the historian's raw materials, created at the time the historian is studying. They are the surviving evidence of past human action and thought—documents, letters, diaries, newspapers, contemporary commentary, even paintings and physical structures from the past. Secondary sources are the work of scholars who have viewed the primary sources and offer their learned judgments on past events, people, and ideas.

## The Primary Sources of Legal History

Because law is written, unlike oral custom, legal historians are blessed with many primary sources. The primary sources have two faces. Public law primary sources tell a story of power. Private law primary sources tell a story of failed agreements and personal harms. Public law is largely the work of legislatures. Private law is largely the preserve of courts.

But the two bundles of sources sometimes include sheaves from one another. A U.S. Supreme Court opinion may settle a suit between one person and another and at the same time announce how the Court will regard all similar suits. The High Court has even been accused of usurping the role of state and federal legislative bodies in making policy decisions, a charge going back to the Court's striking down a law limiting the hours that bakers could work in *Lochner v. New York* (1905). A private lawsuit may involve thousands of individuals and billions of dollars. This is particularly true of "products liability suits" like the Agent Orange, asbestosis, and intrauterine device suits. "Class action suits" in which one case may represent many plaintiffs and many defendants, are common in civil rights litigation, and such litigation often involves public agencies as well as private litigants. Suits against tobacco companies involve both public and private agents, as state attorneys general and Congress have stepped into the litigation.

Public law may aim at particular individuals or organizations, singling them out for punishment or assistance. The very first civil rights acts forbade the costumed evil of the Ku Klux Klan. Congressional "private bills" customarily beginning with the phrase "for the relief of" direct funds and other assistance to cities, companies, and regions. The "bailout" of companies facing bankruptcy like Boeing and A.I.G. and the aid to New Orleans after Hurricane Katrina caused the levees to overflow were private bills. Nothing prevents this crossing over from the public to the private, for public and private are not hard-and-fast categories.

Public law primary sources may appear as part of a "common law" or in a "code." The common-law system originated in England. The king's high courts, based in the medieval town of Westminster, heard and decided cases that came from inferior courts or were brought back to the high courts by their judges when the judges went "on circuit" through the countryside. The High Courts of England were courts of "appeal" or appellate courts. The decisions of the justices of the high courts were recorded and became the basis for a national law, joining the statutes that parliament passed and the king signed, and the king's own royal orders. The decisions of the high courts were sometimes accompanied by opinions of the judges explaining why and how they reached the decisions they did. These decisions, along with the opinions explaining the decisions, were "precedent," applying to all future cases whose facts fit the pattern of the precedent. Thus a body of legal precedent grew. Originally noted by law students and teachers, it was recorded, arranged, and published in commentaries the most famous of which are Chief Justice Edward Coke's exhaustive four-part survey, *Institutes of the Laws of England* (1628), Matthew Hale's *History of the Pleas of the Crown*, a tract on the criminal laws of England, published posthumously in 1736, and William Blackstone's *Commentaries on the Laws of England* (1765–1769), a four-volume work extolling the common law. Note that in their time, these commentaries were secondary sources. Today scholars regard them as primary sources.

After the *Commentaries* were published, every colonial lawyer of any note studied Blackstone. For the common law came to the American colonies. Indeed, even when the crown allowed the colonists to elect their own assemblies and pass laws, the colonial legislators were told not to violate the common law of England. (The technical reason was that most of the colonies' governments were, in English law, municipal chartered corporations, and every corporation charter required that its bylaws not be repugnant to the laws of England.) Even after the new American states declared their independence of the crown, much of the common law relating to commerce, family, inheritance, and land was retained. American law continues to have an English hue, and law schools still teach remnants of old common-law terminology.

Common-law court systems have a pyramidal shape. At the bottom are trial courts, where judges apply the law, and juries or judges (in so-called bench trials) decide facts. Above these are appellate or appeals courts, whose function is to determine whether the law applied in a case below was correct. At the top of the American common law system are supreme courts. Their decisions and the opinions announcing and explaining those decisions are precedent in the same manner that the English high courts' opinions were precedent. The federal Constitution gave to the U.S. Supreme Court jurisdiction to weigh the statutes and the judicial decisions of the states against the federal Constitution. The Supremacy Clause (Article VI, Cl.2) proclaimed, "This Constitution, and the Laws of the United States which shall be made in Pursuance thereof; and all Treaties made, or which shall be made, under the authority of the United States, shall be the supreme Law of the land; and the Judges in every State shall be bound thereby, any Thing in the Constitution or Laws of any State to the Contrary notwithstanding."

The American judicial system is a hybrid of the common law, however. Unlike England, the federal and state governments are based on written constitutions. These simultaneously limit and empower government. Unlike the "English constitution," which in reality is nothing more than the collection of parliamentary and royal enactments and can be changed at the whim of the lawmakers, American constitutions are codelike in their fundamental place in American laws. They are rarely as comprehensive as European codes, however. The federal Constitution, for example, is barely more than 7,500 words. Judges' opinions interpreting those constitutions create a body of precedent in dynamic tension with the text of the constitutions.

Law codes are an alternative to common law. The laws of Hammurabi in ancient Mesopotamia and the laws in the Torah were such codes. The most famous western code is that which Roman emperor Justinian ordered compiled in 529 C.E. It was a compendium of rules from republican Roman and later imperial courts. Along with the code, Justinian ordered preparation of a Digest for judges and Institutes for law students. The code, in varying forms, became the basis for many continental European legal systems, including the French "Code Napoleon." English jurists rejected the code, preferring the common-law system, but could not prevent the absorption of certain concepts from the code. In the early nineteenth century, there was a major effort to codify state laws, primarily to prune elements of English common law and to make the law more egalitarian and easy to understand. Part of that movement was the attempt to merge law and equity. In New York (1848) and California (1850) that movement was successful, in part because the leaders, David Dudley Field and Stephen J. Field, respectively, were such able advocates of the reform.

The Code Napoleon echoes in Louisiana law but there are no codes in American law that precisely duplicate the Continental model. The entire body of federal statutes, with accompanying judicial decisions, is called the *United States Code*, but this is really a compilation more than a code.

Statutes are enactments of a legislature to which executives have acceded (or which are passed over the veto of the chief executives). Legislatures often move much faster than courts. For this reason, some political scientists like Rebecca Zeitlow have argued that legislatures are far more important and reliable guarantors of personal rights than are courts. "The insulation of federal courts from the political process arguably make those courts better suited to protect minorities because courts need not answer to the will of the majority." But as with public and private law, the line between common law and code law is not clear. Courts interpret statutes' meaning, and legislators look to judicial precedent to frame new laws.[1]

During the Gilded Age, most states began to codify their legislative enactments, but before that time, the legislation appeared in the journals published by the state assemblies and senates. States now publish and periodically update state law in codes. Published versions run to dozens of volumes. The federal *Statutes at Large* including all the acts of Congress were published in chronological order until the 1875 codification. The Acts of Congress are still published in chronological order, but the U.S. Code, arranged by subject in fifty titles rather than chronologically, is the authoritative source for statutes. It has grown to many thousands of pages and annual supplements are published by the General Printing Office.

The official primary sources of American legal history also include the decisions of courts of "equity." Because of the system of pleading in courts of equity, they are superb sources. The first court of equity was held by the chancellor of England, the king's personal secretary, in late medieval times. To the chancellor's court came people who pled their case in plain language instead of pleading their case in Latin formulas. There were no trials in the old chancellor's court. Instead, he ordered the taking of depositions and decided the cases himself. Once separate and often rivals, today courts of law and courts of equity are unified. Depositions are part of the "discovery" process that precedes cases and can be immensely useful to the historian.

Unlike much of the primary sources of public law, the primary sources of private law highlight the personal side of law practice in America. Private law includes contracts, torts (civil wrongs), domestic law (marriage, divorce, custody), trusts and estates, property law, intellectual property, and the like. The patterns of American litigation experience—why Americans sue, and who sues whom—are revealed in these sources.

The records of the trial courts and the papers of law offices are the treasury of primary private law sources. The former include the docket books of courts, lists of cases filed by date. When a local court sat in its session of "common pleas," the docket book recorded the court's civil business, stating the parties to the suit and the "gravamen" or claim of the plaintiff against the defendant. The docket books of common pleas also indicate the names of jurors empaneled to hear and decide the case if it went to a jury and the names of counsel.

The files of law firms are not always open to scholars. A long-running controversy over whether lawyer-client privilege survives the death of the client has pitted the American Bar Association (the papers of a law office should never be open to scholars) against the American Historical Association and the Organization of American Historians (after a period of years, when the issues have been settled and the parties gone to their reward, the law firm should be allowed to deposit the papers in archives or libraries). The legal papers of nineteenth-century lawyers like Daniel Webster, Andrew Jackson, and Abraham Lincoln already in print prove how useful such sources can be.

The most common civil cases in early America were disputes over land titles, defamation (slander and libel), and debt. Into the nineteenth century, debt continued a major presence in the docket books, but it was soon rivaled by torts—civil wrongs like negligence, nuisance, and negligent accidents. At first, railroad accidents led the way. By the early twentieth century, however, automobile accidents had taken first place. The dockets grew even fuller, this time with broken marriages, custody battles, and other family matters. A few lawsuits are brought by individuals to force government to act. These "private attorney general" suits, as jurist and judge Jerome Frank called them, have become part of many statutes, including the Clean Air Act and the Clean Water Act. They allow people affected by pollution to stand in the role of the government and sue private industries.

## Secondary Sources

No matter how voluminous, the primary sources of American legal history do not speak for themselves. They reveal, but do not explain, the often puzzling contradictions in the legal past. Secondary sources attempt to explain how the law came to be and how it affects us. They include textbooks of legal history, collections of interpretive essays, narrations of particular cases, detailed and heavily annotated monographs, biographies of elite lawmakers, social and cultural studies of how law worked in everyday life, and law review articles with hundreds of footnotes.

But the array of secondary sources does not fully resolve the complex questions that American legal history poses because the authors do not always agree with one another. I have said that collegiality is a feature of our legal scholarship. The mutually supportive relationships among American legal historians do not preclude such disagreements.

Modern American legal history is remarkably diverse in its approaches and methods. In general, one can see the divisions between certain kinds of analytical schemes. The two most important are doctrinal versus law-and-society and conflict versus consensus. What follows is a very brief sketch of the outlines of these two divisions. They are far more sophisticated than I have portrayed them here, and as is often true of summaries of this kind, would probably not be entirely accepted by the scholars themselves.

The doctrinal or internalist approach, long favored by most law professors, sees law as evolving within itself, as judges, jurists, and lawyers struggle to make the law fit a changing world.

Accounts of law from the inside require specialized language and technical expertise. Comparative law expert and law professor Alan Watson explains: "My often repeated argument [is] that legal development—in the broadest sense of law: the structure of the system, its major divisions, the approach to the sources of law, and the legal rules themselves—owes a great deal to the legal tradition and, to a marked degree, is independent of social, political, and economic factors." The doctrinal or internalist view of legal history tends to focus on the courts rather than the legislatures. Bernard Schwartz, like Watson a law professor, put it this way in his history of American law: "The story of American law is the story of the great lawyers and judges in our past."[2]

Some leading advocates of the internalist school conceptualized the story of law as a succession of periods or stages. Each stage or period will see the rise of a dominant style of judging and lawmaking. In 1960, law professor Karl Llewellyn proposed three major periods of legal thinking that he thought characterized the evolution of American law. Llewellyn's periods were "a way of thought and work . . . an on-going of doctrine . . . slowish [in] movement but striking in style." Most important of all, they were adaptive to "the general and pervasive manner over the country at large." He attributed a "grand style" to the founders and the next two generations. They relied on natural law–based ideas like liberty, freedom, and private property to construct the new nation's foundational legal institutions. In other words, they were instrumentalists, seeing law as a means to a goal of a certain kind of society. The initial period of creativity gave way to a stage he called classical legal formalism, rule bound and self-referring, a way of thinking dominant from the end of the Civil War to the early 1900s. Classical or formalistic thinking saw rules deeply embedded in cases and argued that these rules were themselves embedded in fundamental structures of society, the economy, and politics. Judges couched their opinions in terms of the reason of the law, or what rational men would think. Classical or formal legal thinking privileged judicial over legislative lawmaking, believing that the legislators were too easily swayed by local interests and majority rule. Formalism in turn faced a rising tide of legal realism, a law-school pedagogical movement of which Llewellyn was part. Emerging in the 1920s, realism looked not at how law should function, but how it did function. Part of what might be called the modernist movement, legal realism believed that law was indeterminate and open to policy choices and thus could be a potent source of social and economic reform. Legal realism critiqued formalist judging and was instead skeptical, curious, and grounded in the social sciences and facts.[3]

A product of legal realism, the law-and-society approach insists that legal history is a byproduct of the larger social, political, economic, and cultural life. Law is not autonomous. It is a dependent variable, shaped by change outside of the legal academy, the courts, and the texts. "The central point remains, law is a product of social forces, working in society." If law does not work for that society, it does not have "survival value." The external view of law and society features "a commitment to empirical observation and scientific measurement . . . to objectivity and neutrality." Law and society bids its followers to compile detailed observations about trends and shifts in the practice and impact of law—a study of law from the bottom up, and includes legislators and legislation in its purview.[4]

Law and society does not ignore doctrine, the way that lawyers and judges think, or the importance of technical requirements in the law. But the law-and-society scholar is always asking how the internal workings of the law reflect the needs and demands of the world outside the lawyer's office and the courtroom. An example, from Lawrence Friedman's book on the law of succession: "This book is about the routine and the unusual in that branch of law we call the law of succession . . . about the rights and powers, of the dead hand: control of property, or lack

of control, when the person dies." It is "a social process of enor-
mous importance," but it is also an "arcane field of law."[5]

The ideal, of course, is a combination of doctrinal and law-
and-society approaches, research and analysis on where the
internal touches the external processes of legal change. Indeed,
it may be true that we are all law-and-society scholars now.
Certainly the gap between the internal and the externalist
approaches seems to be closing, as more recent secondary
sources combine both approaches or borrow from both. As
G. Edward White has written of his own journey from first to
third edition of *The American Judicial Tradition*, "In the interval
. . . the interest of scholars, students, and judges in the historical
dimensions of law have grown dramatically, with the result that
I have many more colleagues . . . working on projects in legal
and constitutional history." Their explorations of both doctrine
and social context has broadened his own.[6]

Such a golden mean is so easily realized in the second of the
major divisions among scholars. Unlike doctrinal and law-and-
society strategies, the debate over the relative importance of conflict and consensus is irreconcilable. It is easy to make a case for
conflict as the dominant theme, for American courts are battle-
grounds for opposing advocates, and legislatures are sites of
competing political and economic interests. In the accounts of
these scholars, legal history mirrors the great struggles in the
larger American chronicle. A survey of American legal history
syllabuses on the Web revealed that there was a kind of consensus over which of these conflicts was most important: civil rights,
labor versus capital, and free speech. As jurisprudent Roscoe
Pound wrote in *My Philosophy of Law* (1941), "I think of law as
in one sense a highly specialized form of social control." Pound,
a conservative by the time he wrote these words, had come to
his conclusions through the study of criminal justice systems.
More radical observers of law and criminal justice, for example
Richard Quinney, believed that law was the means for the state

to protect the interests "of the dominant class," thereby insuring that law "was a device for holding down the exploited class."[7]

The case for consensus rests upon assumptions about the larger course of American legal history. James Willard Hurst, the founder of the law-and-society movement and the foremost chronicler of nineteenth century legal development, argued,

> The historic record . . . shows that . . . we used law to foster and protect the growth of private (that is, non-official) associations like the business corporation or religious, political, and social association, to build centers of energy and opinion which might provide counterweights to official power. . . . We used law to define and to implement an idea of constitutionalism as the norm of all secular power. . . . We used law to promote formal definition of values and of appropriate means to implement values.

Law promoted a rational, fair, and efficient process "by which men created social goals and mobilized energies of mind and feeling to move toward their goals."[8]

Consensus does not preclude orderly change. Consider William E. Nelson's tale of the reformation of the New York State Court of Appeals.

> New York case law in the twentieth century . . . reveal[s] a society in which, before the late 1930s, issues of race, ethnicity, religion and gender were virtually never mentioned in judicial decisions. . . . New Yorkers began to follow a path away from the repressive society in the World War II era. . . . They began to reconceptualize social conflict in terms of the power of majorities and the rights of minorities. As they negotiated their new path, people also used law to elaborate in a step-by-step process that

lasted several decades a new ideology in action—an ideology of liberty, quality, human dignity, and entrepreneurial opportunity that today has matured into the hope of the progressive world.

The varied and changing case of judges, lawsuits, and political figures that march through the book follow the upward path toward "liberty, equality, human dignity, and opportunity," if not quite in lockstep, at least as though they know the steps they must take.[9]

## Criticisms of Legal History

It would be disingenuous of me to deny that legal history has critics. Two somewhat specialized types of secondary sources attract this criticism. The first, termed by its critics "law office history," takes two forms. First, it may be the use of historical methods, citations, and examples by lawyers and judges to support their legal arguments. "Many lawyers cannot see any difference at all between law and history, assuming that history is engaged in 'court like' activities of fact-finding and telling, and that historians and lawyers' practices are identical." Because of the limitations of space in legal briefs and judicial opinions, and the demands of their roles that the lawyer or judge come down on one side or another of the issue, law office history of this type often omits nuance and qualification, context and counter-examples.[10]

Historians concerned about the use of history in judicial opinions have on occasion tangled with judges. The most notorious controversy concerned Supreme Court Justice Hugo Black, a voracious reader of history, and Pulitzer Prize–winning historian Leonard Levy. Black thought that the First Amendment barred Congress from punishing political opinions, and said so in his opinions for the Court. Levy's *Legacy of Suppression: Freedom of Speech and Press in Early America* (1960) argued that many of the congressmen who voted for the First Amendment assumed it only barred prior censorship. At the time, Black told mutual friends that he feared that Levy's work would destroy the First Amendment. Levy later wrote that Black "was innocent of history when he did not distort it or invent it." Nonetheless, when Levy revised his book, he changed the title to *The Emergence of a Free Press.*[11]

A second type of law office history subject to much criticism derives from historians acting as expert witnesses. Historians are signed by a law firm to prepare materials supporting their side in a lawsuit. More and more historians are joining this queue. The rewards are considerable—the hourly rate is mid–three figures, and the hours can pile up. At first, historians provided these services without pay. Southern historians John Hope Franklin and C. Vann Woodward and constitutional historian Alfred Kelly helped the NAACP deal with historical questions in *Brown v. Board of Education* (1954). In the 1960s and 1970s, historians worked for lawyers representing Indian tribes in the effort to regain ancestral lands and for states quarreling with one another over boundary lines and water rights. More recently, they have provided research and testified in voting rights (reapportionment) cases and suits involving the dangers of tobacco products, lead paint, and asbestos. There is a corporation that recruits and trains historians for this occupation and supplies their names to law firms. More informal networks within the historical profession helped to recruit the over fifty historians who assist defendants in tobacco litigation.

Historians perform highly useful services as expert witnesses, and some historians called into service as expert witnesses truly believe in their cause. J. Morgan Kousser, who has spent the past two decades testifying for racial minorities in voting rights cases, regards the experience as "affording opportunities to tell the truth and do good at the same time." Other historians were not so pleased with their experience. Alfred Kelly, whose expert witnessing helped the Legal Defense Fund of the NAACP win *Brown v. Board of Education*, later recalled, "Here I was, caught between my own ideals as a historian and what these people [the LDF] in New York wanted and needed." Historian David Rothman explained his own dilemma: "To enter the courtroom is to do many things, but it is not to do history. The essential attributes that we treasure most about historical inquiry must be left outside the courtroom door."[12]

A second criticism of American legal history appears in the work of the Critical Legal Studies movement. The criticism is a powerful one: That mainstream or conventional American legal history is "corrosive," "often wholly unreflecting, unselfconscious," because it accepts the unvarying role of "contingency" in the evolution of law. In other words, mainstream legal history is either too uncritical of the phenomena it describes or an apologist for the existing legal system.[13]

There is some truth to the charge but little merit to its sweep. What may be called "Whig legal histories" (a term borrowed from Herbert Butterfield's indictment of "Whig history") do promote a pollyanna notion of the progress of the law: everything is for the ultimate good; the triumph of right is inevitable; everyone's motives are above reproach. In-house or commissioned histories of law firms or judicial circuits may find much to praise and little to criticize in their subjects. But most academic legal history has outgrown these criticisms. It is complex, sympathetic but not apologetic, and sophisticated.[14]

With Lincoln, I am loath to close. The sources for legal history in the twentieth century exceed those for all previous times in our history. The prospects for scholarship in recent American legal history are correspondingly immense and inviting. The generation that made legal history a staple on bookstore shelves and in college classrooms is becoming history itself, but new generations of scholars are adding cultural and literary insights to older social and economic themes. It is a time of great promise for scholars, students, and everyone interested in American legal history. The shame is that Stephen and Kermit are not here to share the bounty of the field they helped plant.

# Notes

## Introduction: A Nation of Laws

1. President Barack Obama, Address to the Nation, May 21, 2009; full text available at dyn.politico.com/printstory.cfm?uuid=64B1A2 13-18FE-70B2-A8245086E1BF3698.

2. John Adams to William Tudor, December 18, 1816, in Charles Francis Adams, ed., *Works of John Adams* (Boston: Little, Brown, 1856), 10: 233; Adams, *A Defense of the Constitutions of Governments of the United States of America* [1787], in Adams, *Works of Adams* 4: 419.

3. President Obama, Address to the Hispanic Prayer Breakfast, June 19, 2009; http://cnsnews.com/Public/Content/Article.aspx?rsrcid =49832.

## Prologue: Slavery and Race Law

1. Seymour Martin Lipset, *American Exceptionalism: A Double-Edged Sword* (New York: Norton, 1996), 20; *Bolling v. Sharpe* 347 U.S. 479, 499 (1954) (Warren C.J.).

2. Thomas Paine, *The Rights of Man, Common Sense and Other Political Writings* (New York: Oxford University Press, 1998), 34. The text of Jefferson's final draft of the Declaration of Independence is available in a multitude of sources, e.g., David Armitage, *The Declaration of Independence: A Global History* (Cambridge, Mass.: Harvard University Press,

2007), 116. It is also a legal document (actually a "bill in equity"), drawn by a lawyer based on his legal experience. See Peter Charles Hoffer, *The Law's Conscience: Equitable Constitutionalism in America* (Chapel Hill: University of North Carolina Press, 1990), 71–76.

3. George Mason, 1773, in "Abstracts from the Virginia Charters," quoted in Kate Mason Rowland, *The Life of George Mason, 1725–1792* (New York: G. P. Putnam, 1892), 404.

4. Fugitive Slave Law of 1793, *Annals of Congress*, 2nd Congress, 2nd Session, 1793, 1414–1415.

5. Lysander Spooner, *The Unconstitutionality of Slavery* (Boston: 1860), 6, 124; *Commonwealth v. Thomas Aves*, 35 Mass. 193, 210, 211(1836) (Shaw C.J.).

6. Margaret L. Coit, *John C. Calhoun, American Portrait* (Boston: Houghton Mifflin, 1950), 186, 303; John C. Calhoun, Speech on the Reception of Abolitionist Petitions, February 6, 1837, *Congressional Globe* 24th Cong. 2nd Sess., 159.

7. *Dred Scott v. Sanford* 60 U.S. 393, 407 (1857) (Taney C.J.).

8. Ibid. at 754 (McLean J.).

9. Alfred H. Kelly and Winfred E. Harbison, *The American Constitution*, 3rd ed. (New York: Norton, 1963), 360; *Ableman v. Booth*, 62 U.S. 506, 515 (1858) (Taney C.J.).

10. *Plessy v. Ferguson*, 163 U.S. 537, 555 (1896) (Harlan J.).

11. *Brown v. Board of Education*, 347 U.S. 483, 494–495 (1954) (Warren C.J.).

12. Southern Manifesto, *Congressional Record*, 84th Congress, 2nd Sess., (1956), 4515–4516.

## Chapter 1: Contested Categories

1. Daniel T. Rogers, *Contested Truths: Keywords in American Politics since Independence* (New York: Basic Books, 1987), 31. Rogers was referring to the Jacksonian Democrats. I have taken the liberty of extending the reference as it seems to me to be a recurring theme.

2. *Marbury v. Madison* 5 U.S. 137, 179, 176 (1803) (Marshall C.J.).

3. John C. Calhoun, "Exposition" (1828), in Clyde N. Wilson and W. Edwin Hemphill, eds., *The Papers of John C. Calhoun* (Columbia: University of South Carolina Press, 1977), 10: 445, 447, 449, 457, 459, 461, 493, 529, 531, 533; Andrew Jackson, "Proclamation by Andrew

Jackson, President of the United States" (1832), Gilder Lehrman Document collection, www.gilderlehrman.org/search/display_results .php?id=GLC01863.

4. On "background rules," see Anthony J. Bellia Jr. and Bradford R. Clark, "The Federal Common Law of Nations," *Columbia Law Review* 109 (January 2009), 5.

5. AHA Act of Incorporation, January 4, 1889, www.historians .org/info/charter.cfm.

6. Peter Charles Hoffer, *Law and People in Colonial America*, 2nd ed. (Baltimore: Johns Hopkins University Press, 1998), 79–80.

7. Wayne McIntosh, *The Appeal of Civil Law: A Political-Economic Analysis of Litigation* (Urbana: University of Illinois Press, 1990), 191–192; Lawrence Friedman, *American Law in the 20th Century* (New Haven, Conn.: Yale University Press, 2002), 480.

8. P. S. Atiyah, "Tort Law and the Alternatives: Some Anglo-American Comparisons," *Duke Law Journal* 1987 (1987), 1009.

9. Injuryboard, "Tort Reform and the Effect of Medical Malpractice Caps" (June 26, 2002), www.injuryboard.com/help-center/articles/ tort-reform-and-the-effect-of-medical-malpractice-caps.aspx.

10. Arlynn Leiber Presser, "Some Fees Called Unethical: ABA Committee Considers Proposal to Limit Tort Contingencies," *American Bar Association Journal* 80 (April 1994); ABA Task Force on Contingent Fees, "Contingent Fees in Mass Tort Litigation" *Tort and Insurance Law Journal* 42 (2006), 105–189.

11. Garrison explained why he and his *Liberator* supported the suppression of secession in 1861: "because, as between the combatants, there is no wrong or injustice on the side of the government, while there is nothing but violence, robbery, confiscation, perfidy, lynch law, usurpation, and a most diabolical purpose on the side of the secessionists." Wendell Phillips Garrison and Francis Jackson Garrison, *William Lloyd Garrison, 1805–1879: The Story of His Life Told by His Children* (New York: Century, 1889), 4: 26.

12. Ida B. Wells, "Our Country's National Crime Is Lynching" (1892), in Michelle Diane Wright, ed., *Broken Utterances: A Selected Anthology of 19th Century Black Women's Social Thought* (Baltimore: Three Sistahs Press, 2007), 277; Jesse P. Guzman, ed., *1952 Negro Yearbook* (New York: William H. Wise, 1952), 275–279.

13. Philip J. Ethington, *The Public City: The Political Construction of*

*Urban Life in San Francisco, 1850–1900* (Berkeley: University of California Press, 2001), 130–137.

14. Regulus [Herman Husband], *A Fan for Fanning and a Touchstone to Tryon, Containing an Impartial Account of the Rise and Progress of the Much Talked about Regulation in North-Carolina* (Boston, 1771), 14.

15. Henry David Thoreau, "Resistance to Civil Government" (1849), in *The Writings of Henry David Thoreau* (Boston: Houghton, Mifflin, 1937), 792.

16. The "Mayflower Compact" (1620), http://avalon.law.yale.edu/17th_century/mayflower.asp.

17. David Campbell, "Sketch of the Hardships Endured by Those Who Crossed the Plains in '46" (1910), in "Diaries, Memoirs, Letters and Reports along the Trails West" at http://lib-operations.sonoma.edu/fin/aaa-0712.html.

18. *Friedman v. Gomel Chesed Hebrew Cemetery Ass'n*, Superior Court of New Jersey, Chancery Division, 22 N.J. Super. 544, 547 (1952).

19. *Yome v. Gorman*, 242 N.Y. 395, 403 (1926) (Cardozo C.J.).

20. Thomas Jefferson to Danbury Baptist Association, January 1, 1802, Thomas Jefferson, *The Writings of Thomas Jefferson* (Washington, D.C.: Taylor and Maury, 1859), 8: 113.

21. *Church of the Holy Trinity v. United States*, 143 U.S. 457, 468, 471(1892) (Brewer, J.); William Addison Blakely et al., *American State Papers Bearing on Sunday Legislation* (Washington, D.C.: Religious Liberty Association, 1911), 488 n.2.

22. *Van Orden v. Perry*, 545 U.S. 677, 683, 684 (2005) (Rehnquist C.J.).

23. Id. at 709 (Stevens J.).

24. Sarah Barringer Gordon, "Law and Religion, 1720–1920" in Christopher Tomlins and Michael Grossberg, eds., *Cambridge History of American Law* (New York: Cambridge University Press, 2008), 2: 448.

25. Kenneth L. Karst, *Law's Promise, Law's Expression* (New Haven, Conn.: Yale University Press, 1995), 168.

26. Barack Obama, *Dreams from My Father: A Story of Race and Inheritance* (New York: Times Books, 1995), viii.

27. *Wong Kim Ark v. U.S.* 169 U.S. 649, 674–675 (1898) (Gray J.).

28. *Chae Chan Ping v. U.S.* (The Chinese Exclusion Case), 130 U.S. 581, 595 (1889) (Field J.); Lucy Salyer, *Laws Harsh as Tigers: Chinese Immigrants and the Shaping of Modern Immigration Law* (Chapel Hill: University of North Carolina Press, 1995), 79.

29. Mark S. Weiner, *Americans without Law: The Racial Boundaries of Citizenship* (New York: New York University Press, 2006), 72.

30. The poem is the work of poet Emma Lazarus, "The New Colossus" (1883), a part of which was inscribed on the Statue of Liberty in 1912.

31. Zoe Lofgren, "Globalization, Security, and Human Rights: Immigration in the Twenty-First Century, A Decade of Radical Change in Immigration Law, an Insider's Perspective," *Stanford Law and Policy Review* 16 (2005), 349–378; Julia Preston, "Obama to Push Immigration Bill as One Priority," *New York Times*, April 8, 2009, A1.

32. Robert C. McMath, *American Populism: A Social History 1877–1898* (New York: Hill and Wang, 1990), 23, 138.

33. For example, the anti-Masonic movement "served as a catalyst for the formation of the first true mass party organizations in the United States." Ronald P. Formisano, *For the People: American Populist Movements from the Revolution to the 1850s* (Chapel Hill: University of North Carolina Press, 2007), 91.

34. Cass Sunstein, *The Rule of Law in America* (Baltimore: Johns Hopkins University Press, 2001), 27, 31.

35. Thomas K. McGraw, *Prophets of Regulation: Charles Francis Adams, Louis D. Brandeis, James M. Landis, Alfred E. Kahn* (Cambridge, Mass.: Harvard University Press, 1984), 213; Landis quoted at 214; W. F. Willoughby, *The Principles of Judicial Administration* (Washington, D.C.: Brookings, 1927), 21; Philip K. Howard, *The Death of Common Sense: How Law Is Suffocating America* (New York: Random House, 1994), 10, 11.

## Chapter 2: Divergent Paths

1. Oliver Wendell Holmes Jr., "The Path of the Law" *Harvard Law Review* 10 (1897), 458.

2. Nicholas Wade, "A Mind Still Prescient after All These Years" *New York Times*, February 10, 2009, D1; Tim M. Berra, *Charles Darwin: The Concise Story of an Extraordinary Man* (Baltimore: Johns Hopkins University Press, 2009), 1.

3. Charles Darwin, *On the Origin of the Species* [1859], 6th corrected ed. (New York: Appleton, 1900), 2: 267.

4. Stephen Jay Gould, "Evolution's Erratic Pace" *Natural History*

86 (May 1977), 12; Gould, *The Structure of Evolutionary Theory*, 6th ed. (Cambridge, Mass.: Harvard University Press, 2002), 1019; Michael Kammen, *People of Paradox: An Inquiry concerning the Origins of American Civilization* (New York: Knopf, 1973), 89.

5. Richard J. Dawkins, *The Selfish Gene*, 3rd ed. (New York: Oxford University Press, 2006), 33, 197.

6. William Blackstone, *Commentaries on the Laws of England* [1759–1765] (London: Bancroft-Whitney, 1915), 1: 67, 69.

7. Eugene Genovese, *The World the Slaveholders Made: Two Essays in Interpretation*, rev. ed. (Middletown, Conn: Wesleyan University Press, 1988), 227, 228.

8. Lawrence Friedman, *A History of American Law*, 3rd ed. (New York: Simon & Schuster, 2005), 255; Grant Gilmore, *The Ages of American Law* (New Haven, Conn.: Yale University Press, 1974), 10.

9. Christopher L. Tomlins, *The State and the Unions: Labor Relations, Law, and the Organized Labor Movement in America, 1880–1960* (New York: Cambridge University Press, 1985), 305.

10. Richard A. Epstein, "What's Good for Pharma Is Good for America" *Boston Globe,* December 3, 2006, E1.

11. Fractal theory states that big things are composed of smaller versions of themselves. Look at the branches of a tree. Then look at the veins of a leaf from the tree. They are similar. Examine the bronchial tubes in our lungs. Then use a microscope to look at the blood vessels that supply the bronchial tubes. They reproduce the form of the bronchial tubes. The notion is the work of Benoit Mandelbrot, see *The Fractal Geometry of Nature* (San Francisco: W. H. Freeman, 1982). A popular version appears in James Gleick, *Chaos: Making a New Science* (New York: Viking, 1987).

12. On the notion of instrumentalism, with all its implications for the way that powerful interests can find their friends in the courts, see Morton Horwitz, *The Transformation of the Law, 1780–1860* (Cambridge, Mass.: Harvard University Press, 1977), 4, 31; quotation at 155. But see Peter S. Karsten, *Heart versus Head: Judge-Made Law in Nineteenth-Century America* (Chapel Hill: University of North Carolina Press, 1997), 206: "the creation of . . . doctrine . . . amounted to a 'kindler, gentler' instrumentalism. . . . As such, its story is further evidence of the bankruptcy of the claims that nineteenth-century jurists were pro-

entrepreneurial instrumentalists," men whose heads denied their hearts' desire to help the helpless.

13. Joel F. Handler, *Law and the Search for Community* (Philadelphia: University of Pennsylvania Press, 1990), 156.

14. Hendrik Hartog, *Man and Wife in America: A History* (Cambridge, Mass.: Harvard University Press, 2000), 304, 305.

15. John Adams, quoted in John E. Ferling, *John Adams: A Life* (New York: Macmillan, 1996), 153.

16. Bernard Bailyn, *Ideological Origins of the American Revolution*, rev. ed. (Cambridge, Mass.: Harvard University Press, 1992), 231.

17. *MacPherson v. Buick*, 217 N.Y. 382, 391(1916) (Cardozo J.).

18. G. Edward White, *Tort Law in America: An Intellectual History*, expanded ed. (New York: Oxford University Press, 2003), 120, 168–169.

19. Louis D. Brandeis and Samuel D. Warren, "The Right to Privacy," *Harvard Law Review* 4 (1890), 195, 199.

20. *Griswold v. Connecticut*, 381 U.S. 479, 484 (1965) (Douglas J.).

21. John Adams, "A Defense of the Constitutions of the United States" (1787), in Charles Francis Adams, ed., *The Works of John Adams* (Boston: Little, Brown, 1851), 6: 9; Frank I. Michelman, "Takings, 1987," *Columbia Law Review* 88 (1988), 126.

22. Charles Loring Brace, *The Dangerous Classes of New York and Twenty Years' Work among Them* (New York: Wyncoop, 1872), ii; Brace to Miss G. Schyler (1877), in Emma Brace, ed., *The Life of Charles Loring Brace, Told Chiefly through His Letters* (New York: Scribners, 1894), 355.

23. Michelman, "Takings, 1987," 1627–1628.

24. Richard W. Bauman, *Ideology and Community in the First Wave of Critical Legal Studies* (Toronto: University of Toronto Press, 2003), 102.

## Chapter 3: Adversaries and Partisans

1. *Tinker v. Des Moines Independent School District*, 393 U.S. 503 (1969); *Meritor Savings Bank v. Vinson*, 477 U.S. 57 (1986); *Mapp v. Ohio*, 367 U.S. 643 (1961); Myron Levin, "Widow's Legal Battle with Philip Morris Ends," *Los Angeles Times*, March 21, 2006, C1.

2. Peter Charles Hoffer, *Law and People in Colonial America*, 2nd ed. (Baltimore: Johns Hopkins University Press, 1998), 81.

3. Marc Galanter, "Explaining Litigation," *Law and Society Review* 9 (1975), 347–357.

4. John M. Conley and William M. O'Barr, *Rules versus Relationships: The Ethnography of Legal Discourse* (Chicago: University of Chicago Press, 1990), 130.

5. Marc Galanter, *Lowering the Bar: Lawyer Jokes and Legal Culture* (Madison: University of Wisconsin Press, 2006), 130; Lawrence Friedman, *Total Justice* (New York: Russell Sage, 1994), 17.

6. Burnita Shelton Matthews, "The Woman Juror," *Women's Lawyers Journal* 15 (1927), 3; *New York Times*, October 24, 1909, A1.

7. Alan Dershowitz, *Reasonable Doubts: The Criminal Justice System and the O. J. Simpson Case* (New York: Simon and Schuster, 1997), 79.

8. The law student was the author's son, Williamjames Hoffer. Law students might have been expected to show some impassivity, but the nation did not. See "Sobbing, Elation at Simpson Verdict," October 3, 1995, CNN, www.cnn.com/US/OJ/verdict/reaction/ index.html; Dershowitz, *Reasonable Doubts*, 11.

9. Fred Rodell, *Woe unto You, Lawyers*, rev. ed. (New York: Berkley, 1980), 1.

10. The quotation from Alexis de Tocqueville appears in his *Democracy in America* (1830–1837), translated and edited by Harvey C. Mansfield and Delba Winthrop (Chicago: University of Chicago Press, 2000), 257.

11. The study of the Chicago bar appears in Richard L. Abel, *American Lawyers* (New York: Oxford University Press, 1989), 42.

12. Baldwin quotes in Jerold S. Auerbach, *Unequal Justice: Lawyers and Social Change in Modern America* (New York: Oxford University Press, 1977), 63.

13. Clarence Darrow, *The Story of My Life* (New York: Scribners, 1932), 175.

14. Clarence Darrow, Address to the Jury, August 16, 1912, excerpted in Arthur Weinberg, ed., *Attorney for the Damned: Clarence Darrow in the Courtroom* (Chicago: University of Chicago Press, 1957), 495.

15. Kevin Tierney, *Darrow: A Biography* (New York: Crowell, 1979), 439.

16. John W. Davis to James Byrnes, December 23, 1952, quoted in William H. Harbaugh, *Lawyer's Lawyer: The Life of John W. Davis* (New York: Oxford University Press, 1973), 495.

17. John W. Davis oral argument in *Briggs v. Elliott* (1954), quoted in Richard Kluger, *Simple Justice* (New York: Knopf, 1976), 670–671.

18. Vaishalee Mishra, "Women Lawyers Still Fighting for Equity" Women's Enews, July 19, 2001, http://womensenews.org/article.cfm/dyn/ aid/569/context/archive; Wendy Werner, "Where Have All the Women Attorneys Gone?" Law Practice Today, May 2004, American Bar Association, http://abanet.org/lpm/lpt/articles/mgto 5041.html; Foltz quoted in Barbara Allen Babcock, "Clara Shortridge Foltz: 'First Woman,'" *Valparaiso University Law Review* 28 (1994), 1232; Sandra Day O'Connor, *The Majesty of the Law: Recollection of a Supreme Court Justice* (New York: Random House, 2004), 158; Cynthia Fuchs Epstein, *Women in Law* (New York: Basic Books, 1981), 381; Virginia Drachman, *Sisters in Law: Women Lawyers in Modern American History* (Cambridge, Mass.: Harvard University Press, 1998), 241; Bernard F. Lentz and David N. Laband, *Sex Discrimination in the Legal Profession* (Westport: Quorum, 1995), 18; Charlie Savage, "Wider World of Choices to Fill Souter's Vacancy," *New York Times*, May 2, 2009, A1.

19. American Bar Association Commission on Racial and Ethnic Diversity, www.abanet.org/minorities; American Civil Liberties Union, www.aclu.org/about.

20. Harry S. Truman, Whistle Stop Speech in Elizabeth, New Jersey, October 7, 1948, in William Safire, ed., *Lend Me Your Ears: Great Speeches in History*, 3rd ed. (New York: Norton, 2004), 960.

21. Information on Georgia's assembly from www.legis.state.ga.us/legis/2007_08/senate and from www.legis.state.ga.us/legis/2009_10/house/bios; information on members of Congress from www .house.gov and www.senate.gov.

22. Not a rhetorical question. In many states, domestic courts, traffic courts, courts of small claims, and so-called magistrates courts are presided over by nonlawyers.

23. Richard Perez-Pena, "The Nation: Making Law vs. Making Money; Lawyers Abandon Legislatures for Greener Pastures," *New York Times*, February 21, 1999, Week in Review, p. 3.

24. Library of Congress, Public Laws for the 109th Congress, http://thomas.loc.gov/bss/d109/d109laws.html; Hoffer, *Law and People*, 89; *New York Times*, February 28, 1897, A1; Moisei Iakovlevich Ostrogorskii, *Democracy and the Party System in the United States: A Study in Extra-constitutional Government* (New York, Macmillan, 1910), 373.

25. Harvard Law School, New First Year Curriculum, October 6, 2006, www.law.harvard.edu/news/2006/10/06_curriculum.php.

26. William D. Popkin, *Statutes in Court: The History and Theory of Statutory Interpretation* (Durham: Duke University Press, 1999), 62; Randall M. Miller and William Pencak, *Pennsylvania: A History of the Commonwealth* (College Park, Pa.: Pennsylvania State University Press, 2002), 252; Guido Calabresi, *A Common Law for the Age of Statutes* (Cambridge, Mass.: Harvard University Press, 1982), 1.

27. Gary Slapper and David Kelly, *The English Legal System*, 6th ed. (London: Routledge, 2003), 14, 15, 16.

28. John G. Stewart, "The Civil Rights Act of 1964, Tactics," in Robert D. Loevy, ed., *The Civil Rights Act of 1964: The Passage of the Law That Ended Racial Segregation* (Albany, N.Y.: SUNY Press, 1997), 211–320.

29. Morton Horwitz, *The Transformation of the Law, 1780–1860* (Cambridge, Mass.: Harvard University Press, 1977), 256–257.

30. New Jersey Courts Online, "Court Administration"; www.judiciary.state .nj.us/admin.htm; accessed May 2, 2009; California Trial Court Roster, updated April 8, 2009, www.courtinfo.ca.gov/courts/trial/judges.htm; North Dakota District Court Judges, accessed May 2, 2009; www.ndcourts.com/court/Districts/Judges.htm.

31. Data from Karen O'Connor and Larry J. Sabato, *American Government, Continuity and Change* (New York: Longman, 2003) 345; "Bankruptcy Filings Up in Calendar Year 2008," U.S. courts news service, www.uscourts.gov/Press_Releases/2009/BankruptcyFilingsDec 2008.cfm.

32. *Smith v. Oregon*, 494 U.S. 872 (1990); *City of Boerne v. Flores*, 521U.S. 507 (1997). See generally Carolyn N. Long, *Religious Freedom and Indian Rights: The Case of Smith v. Oregon* (Lawrence: University Press of Kansas, 2000), 203–279.

33. Richard Posner, *How Judges Think* (Cambridge, Mass.: Harvard University Press, 2008), 2, 28; Robert Keeton, *Judging* (St. Paul, Minn.: West, 1990), 15.

34. Keeton, *Judging*, 15; *Prigg v. Pennsylvania*, 41U.S. 539, 610 (1841) (Story J.). Story letter quoted in Robert Cover, *Justice Accused: Anti-Slavery and the Judicial Process* (New Haven, Conn.: Yale University Press, 1984), 119.

35. Cover, *Justice Accused*, 240; Henry J. Abraham, *Justices, Presi-*

*dents, and Senators: A History of the U.S. Supreme Court Appointments from Washington to Clinton* (Lanham, Md.: Rowman and Littlefield, 1999), 328.

36. G. Edward White, *American Judicial Tradition: Profiles of Leading American Judges* (New York: Oxford University Press, 1976), 188, 274; Posner, *How Judges Think*, 27, 65.

37. Peter Charles Hoffer, Williamjames Hull Hoffer, and N. E. H. Hull, *The Supreme Court: An Essential History* (Lawrence: University Press of Kansas, 2007), 2–6, 34–35. Field and Douglas were not untoward in their ambition. In fact, of the forty-four men to hold the nation's highest office as of 2009, twenty-six had legal training and practiced as lawyers. Among those who ran for president and lost, eighteen were lawyers. Norman Gross, ed., *America's Lawyer-Presidents* (Chicago: American Bar Association, 2009).

38. Lucas A. Powe, "The Supreme Court and Election Returns," in Christopher Tomlins, ed., *The United States Supreme Court: The Pursuit of Justice* (Boston: Houghton Mifflin, 2005), 423–445. Another version of this is that "courts are broadly in step with public opinion," Jeffrey Rosen, *The Most Democratic Branch: How Courts Serve America* (New York: Oxford University Press, 2006), xii. The problem with this generalization occurs when public opinion is badly split on an issue, like slavery or affirmative action. The relative impact of doctrinal development and outside political pressure on the Court is the subject of an ongoing debate among legal scholars and historians. See "Forum: The Debate over the Constitutional Revolution of 1937," in *American Historical Review* 110 (2005), 1046–1115, with essays by G. Edward White, William E. Leuchtenberg, and Laura Kalman.

39. Albert Beveridge, *The Life of John Marshall* (Boston: Houghton Mifflin, 1919) 3: 195–196; Peter Charles Hoffer, *The Treason Trials of Aaron Burr* (Lawrence: University Press of Kansas, 2008), 172–178.

40. O'Neall quotations in Michael Stephen Hindus, "Black Justice under White Law: Criminal Prosecutions of Blacks in Antebellum South Carolina," *Journal of American History* 63 (1976), 578; *McReady v. Thomson*, 23 S.C.L. (1Dud.) 131, 134 (1838); and Lillian A. Kibler, "Unionist Sentiment in South Carolina in 1860," *Journal of South History* 4 (1938), 350–351, 360.

41. Auerbach, *Unequal Justice*, 71; Laura Kalman, *Abe Fortas: A Biography* (New Haven, Conn.: Yale University Press, 1990), 337; Stan-

ley I. Kutler, *The Wars of Watergate: The Last Crisis of Richard M. Nixon* (New York: Norton, 1992), 149–150.

42. Arthur E. Sutherland, *The Law at Harvard: A History of Men and Ideas, 1817–1967* (Cambridge, Mass.: Harvard University Press, 1967), 214–215; *The AALS Directory of Law School Teachers, 2006–2007* (St. Paul, Minn.: Thompson West, 2008), 71–73.

43. Rodell, *Woe*, 8–9. John Osborn Jr.'s 1970 novel *Paper Chase* and Scott Turow's semi-documentary *One L* (1979), both set at Harvard Law School, where Osborn and Turow spent three eventful years of their lives, are revelatory but may not be entirely representative of legal education today. Today even HLS wears a kinder, gentler face.

44. Michael Hoeflich, *Selling the Law in Antebellum America: The Production and Distribution of Law Books, 1780–1870* (New Castle, Del.: Oak Knoll Press, 2008); chapter 3 describes the book sales.

45. C. C. Langdell, *A Selection of Cases on the Law of Contracts* (Cambridge, Mass., 1871), vii; William P. LaPiana, *Logic and Experience: The Origin of Modern Legal Education* (New York: Oxford University Press, 1994), 16 and after.

46. On contracts teaching and theory in the law schools, controversies, and all, see F. H. Buckley, ed., *The Fall and Rise of Freedom of Contract* (Durham, N.C.: Duke University Press, 1999), 3–4 and after.

47. John Henry Schlegel, *American Legal Realism and Empirical Social Science* (Chapel Hill: University of North Carolina Press, 1995), 66; Laura Kalman, *Legal Realism at Yale, 1927–1960* (Chapel Hill: University of North Carolina Press, 1986), 26; 47, 60.

48. The term "progressive pragmatist" comes from N. E. H. Hull, *Roscoe Pound and Karl Llewellyn: Searching for an American Jurisprudence* (Chicago: University of Chicago Press, 1997), 7.

49. Hull, *Pound and Llewellyn*, 156; Frankfurter to Walter Lippmann, May 11, 1927, Felix Frankfurter Papers, Harvard Law School.

50. Pound to Walter Lippmann, January 26, 1927, quoted in Hull, *Pound and Llewellyn*, 159; Charles Clark to Felix Frankfurter, April 27, 1927, Frankfurter Papers; Charles Clark to Harrison T. Sheldon, May 12, 1927, Charles E. Clark Papers, Yale University Library.

51. Clark to Sheldon; Wigmore quoted in Hull, *Pound and Llewellyn*, 157.

52. Karl Llewellyn, "Some Realism about Realism," *Harvard Law Review* 44 (1931) 1222; William W. Fisher III, Morton Horwitz, and

Thomas A. Reed, eds., *American Legal Realism* (New York: Oxford University Press, 1993), xiii; Hull, *Pound and Llewellyn*, 14–15; Schlegel, *American Legal Realism*, 257.

53. Charlie Savage and Scott Shane, "Terror-War Fallout Lingers over Bush Lawyers," *New York Times*, March 9, 2009, A1; Mark Mazetti and David Johnston, "Bush Weighed Using Military in Arrests," *New York Times*, July 24, 2009, A1.

## *Chapter 4: Criminal Trials*

1. Robert S. Bennett quoted in Kim Eisner, "Robert Bennett Throws Punches, Tells Tales," January 30, 2008, www.washingtonian .com/blogarticles/people/capitalcomment/6301.html. If homicide is any guide to trial rates: Gary Lafree and Andromachi Tseloni, "Democracy and Crime: A Multilevel of Homicide Trends in Forty-four Countries, 1950–2000," *Annals of the American Academy of Political and Social Science* 605 (2006), 26–56; Franklin E. Zimring and Gordon Hawkins, *Crime Is Not the Problem: Lethal Violence in America* (New York: Oxford University Press, 1997), 61–72, 209.

2. Karl N. Llewellyn and E. Adamson Hoebel, *The Cheyenne Way: Conflict and Case Law in Primitive Jurisprudence* (Norman: University of Oklahoma Press, 1941), 21. Out of the top twenty-five legal-themed shows on television, according to the *ABA Journal*, the following featured criminal trials, many for homicide: 1. *L.A. Law* (1986–1994), 2. *Perry Mason* (1957–1966), 3. *The Defenders* (1961–1965), 4. *Law & Order* (1990–present), 7. *Rumpole of the Bailey* (1978–1992), 8. *Boston Legal* (2004–2008), 10. *Night Court* (1984–1992), 12. *Owen Marshall: Counselor at Law* (1971–1974), 13. *JAG* (1995–2005), 14. *Shark* (2006–2008), 18. *Murder One* (1995–1997), 19. *Matlock* (1986–1995), 20. *Reasonable Doubts* (1991–1993), 22. *Judd for the Defense* (1967–1969), and 24. *Petrocelli* (1974–1976). www.abajournal.com/magazine/2009/08.

3. Daniel Givelber, "Lost Innocence: Data and Speculation about the Acquitted," *American Criminal Law Review* 42 (2005), 1172–1173.

4. Narrative here and after from Peter Charles Hoffer, *The Salem Witchcraft Trials: A Legal History* (Lawrence: University Press of Kansas, 1998), 35–53, 94–107, and Hoffer, *The Devil's Disciples: Makers of the Salem Witchcraft Trials* (Baltimore: Johns Hopkins University Press, 1996), 102–178.

5. Examination of Rebecca Nurse, March 24, 1692, in Stephen Nissenbaum and Paul Boyer, eds., *The Salem Witchcraft Papers: Verbatim Transcripts of the Legal Documents of the Salem Witchcraft Outbreak of 1692* (New York: Da Capo, 1977) 1: 180, and George Lincoln Burr., ed., *Narratives of the New England Witchcraft Cases* (New York: Scribners, 1914), 158–159.

6. Quotations from *The Life, Trial, and Execution of Captain John Brown* . . . (New York: De Witt, 1859), archived at www.yale.edu/lawweb/avalon/treatise/john_brown/john_brown.htm.

7. Alexander Stuart quoted in Edward L. Ayers, *In the Presence of Mine Enemies: War in the Heart of America, 1859–1863* (New York: Norton, 2003), 50; South Carolina Secession Ordinance in Charleston, South Carolina, *Courier*, December 24, 1860.

8. Susan B. Anthony to Elizabeth Cady Stanton, November 5, 1872, quoted in Lynn Sherr, ed., *The Trial of Susan B. Anthony* (1874), reprinted (Amherst, N.Y.: Humanity Books, 2003), xiv.

9. Quotations from Sherr, *The Trial of Susan B. Anthony*, 62–63, 82.

10. Citizenship Act of March 2, 1907, sec. 3.

11. *MacKenzie v. Hare*, 239 U.S. 299, 311(1915) (McKenna J.).

12. Susan B. Anthony to Elizabeth Cady Stanton, December 2, 1898, in Ellen Carol Dubois, ed., *The Elizabeth Cady Stanton–Susan B. Anthony Reader*, rev. ed. (Boston: Northeastern University Press, 1992), 289.

13. Edward J. Larson, *Summer for the Gods: The Scopes Trial and America's Continuing Debate over Science and Religion* (New York: Basic Books, 1997), 73.

14. Darrow's examination of Bryan's views: www.law.umkc.edu/faculty/projects/ftrials/scopes/day7.htm.

15. *Epperson v. Arkansas*, 393 U.S. 97, 106 (1968) (Fortas J.).

## Chapter 5: Critical Episodes

1. Not all textbooks suffer from this myopia. One counterexample stands out. Robert A. Divine, Timothy H. Breen, George Fredrickson, H. W. Brands, Ariela Gross, and R. Hal Williams, *America Past and Present*, 8th ed. (New York: Longman/Prentice Hall, 2007), has "law and society" essays in each chapter.

2. On the Stono Rebellion: Peter H. Wood, *Black Majority: Negroes*

*in Colonial South Carolina from the 1670s through the Stono Rebellion* (New York: Norton, 1974), 308–330; John K. Thornton, "African Dimensions of the Stono Rebellion," *American Historical Review* 96 (1991), 1102; Mark M. Smith, "Remembering Mary, Shaping Revolt: Reconsidering the Stono Rebellion," *Journal of Southern History* 67 (2001), 513–534. But see Peter Charles Hoffer, *The "Unhappy Accident" at Stono: The Story of a Colonial South Carolina Slave Rebellion,* forthcoming from Oxford University Press, for the version of the core story offered here.

3. South Carolina, Slave Code of 1740, Article 33, *The Public Laws of the State of South Carolina, from Its First Establishment . . .* (Philadelphia: Aitken, 1790), 171.

4. On Seneca Falls: Daniel Walker Howe, *What Hath God Wrought: The Transformation of America, 1815–1848* (New York: Oxford University Press, 2007), 236–237, 849, 872.

5. Elizabeth Cady Stanton, *A History of Woman Suffrage* (Rochester, N.Y.: Fowler and Wells, 1889) 1: 70–71; Eleanor Flexner and Ellen Fitzpatrick, *Century of Struggle: The Woman's Rights Movement in the United States,* enlarged ed. (Cambridge, Mass.: Harvard University Press, 1975), 72.

6. Ruth Rosen, *The World Split Open: How the Modern Women's Movement Changed America* (New York: Viking, 2000), 344.

7. On Calhoun and the California Compromise: Sean Wilentz, *The Rise of American Democracy: Jefferson to Lincoln* (New York: Norton, 2005), 639, 640.

8. John C. Calhoun, Speech on the Fugitive Slave Act of 1850, March 4, 1850, *Congressional Globe,* 31st Cong., 1st Sess. (Senate), 451.

9. Fugitive Slave Act of 1850, passed September 18, 1850, 9 U.S. Stat. 462.

10. Thomas R. R. Cobb, *An Inquiry into the Law of Negro Slavery in the United States of America* (1858), ed. Paul Finkelman (Athens: University of Georgia Press, 1999), 219.

11. H. W. Brands, *Traitor to His Class: The Privileged Life and Radical Presidency of Franklin Delano Roosevelt* (New York: Doubleday, 2008), 43–46.

12. Franklin D. Roosevelt, "First Inaugural Address" March 4, 1933, in "American Rhetoric," at www.americanrhetoric.com/speeches/fdrfirstinaugural.html.

13. On Roosevelt's first inaugural: David M. Kennedy, *Freedom from*

*Fear: The American People in Depression and War, 1929-1945* (New York, Oxford University Press, 1999), 137, on the ultimate assessment of the New Deal, 380.

14. On the packing of the Court: Bruce Ackerman, *We The People Volume 1: Transformations* (Cambridge, Mass.: Harvard University Press, 1991), 257; G. Edward White, *The Constitution and the New Deal* (Cambridge, Mass.: Harvard University Press, 2002), 27 and after; Barry Cushman, *Rethinking the New Deal Court: The Structure of a Constitutional Revolution* (New York: Oxford University Press, 1998), 11-26; William E. Leuchtenberg, *The Supreme Court Reborn: The Constitutional Revolution in the Age of Roosevelt* (New York: Oxford University Press, 1995), 82-162.

15. On Lincoln's first inaugural address: Wilentz, *Rise of American Democracy*, 783, 782.

16. Abraham Lincoln, First Inaugural Address, March 4, 1861, in James M. O'Neill, *Models of Speech Composition* (New York: Century, 1921), 476-481. On Lincoln as lawyer during the secession crisis, see Mark E. Steiner, *An Honest Calling: The Law Practice of Abraham Lincoln* (DeKalb: Northern Illinois University Press, 2009), 177.

## Chapter 6: Discursive Spaces

1. Oliver Wendell Holmes Jr., "The Law," Address to the Suffolk Bar Association, February 5, 1885, in Max Lerner, ed., *The Mind and Faith of Justice Holmes* (Garden City, N.Y.: Halcyon, 1948), 29.

2. Bruce Ackerman called the founding, Reconstruction, and the New Deal "publian moments" in the law. Ackerman, *We the People: Foundations* (Cambridge, Mass.: Harvard University Press, 1991), 41.

3. *Schenck v. U.S.*, 249 U.S. 47, 52 (1918) (Holmes J.).

4. *Abrams v. U.S.*, 250 U.S. 616, 628, 630 (1919) (Holmes J. dissenting).

5. David Rabban, *Free Speech in Its Forgotten Years, 1879-1920* (New York: Cambridge University Press, 1997), 335.

6. William E. Leuchtenberg, *The Supreme Court Reborn: The Constitutional Revolution in the Age of Roosevelt* (New York: Oxford University Press, 1995), 82-118.

7. Barbara Ann Perry, *The Priestly Tribe: The Supreme Court's Image in the American Mind* (Westport, Conn: Greenwood, 1999), 18-19; Peter

Irons, *New Deal Lawyers* (Princeton, N.J.: Princeton University Press, 1993), 276.

8. Was the sharp turn in Owen Roberts's vote the mark of an evolution begun years earlier or his desire to please or the politics looming behind the packing plan? Barry Cushman, *Rethinking the New Deal Court: The Structure of a Constitutional Revolution* (New York: Oxford University Press, 1998), 30–31, thinks the former, while Irons, *New Deal Lawyers*, 279, prefers the latter.

9. Jeffrey Rosen, *The Supreme Court: The Personalities and Rivalries That Defined America* (New York: Macmillan, 2007), 138, 140; Gerald T. Dunne, *Hugo Black and the Judicial Revolution* (New York: Simon and Schuster, 1978), 51.

10. Lawrence Friedman, *American Law in the 20th Century* (New Haven, Conn.: Yale University Press, 2002), 160; Joseph Rauh quoted in Katie Louchheim, ed., *The Making of the New Deal: The Insiders Speak* (Cambridge, Mass.: Harvard University Press, 1984), 58.

11. David J. Garrow, *Bearing the Cross: Martin Luther King, Jr., and the Southern Christian Leadership Conference* (New York: Morrow, 1986), 274.

12. Martin Luther King Jr., "Letter from Birmingham City Jail, April 16, 1963," quoted in Clayborne Carson, ed., *The Eyes on the Prize Civil Rights Reader* (New York: Penguin, 1991), 153; NAACP source quoted in Michael Klarman, *From Jim Crow to Civil Rights: The Supreme Court and the Struggle for Racial Equality* (New York: Oxford University Press, 2004), 379.

13. See N. E. H. Hull and Peter Charles Hoffer, Roe v. Wade: *The Abortion Rights Controversy in American History* (Lawrence: University Press of Kansas, 2001), 135–180.

14. Hull and Hoffer, *Roe v. Wade*, 248–256.

15. *Planned Parenthood v. Casey* 505 U.S. 833, 843, 846 (Kennedy J.) (1992).

16. 505 U.S. at 854–855, 866, 867, 868 (Souter J.).

17. 505 U.S. at 713 (O'Connor J.).

18. Jeffrey Toobin, *The Run of His Life: The People v. O. J. Simpson* (New York: Random House, 1996), 12.

19. Vincent Bugliosi, *Outrage: The Five Reasons Why O. J. Simpson Got Away with Murder* (New York: Norton, 1996), 262.

20. Ibid., 270.

21. Ibid., 276, 277.

22. Alan M. Dershowitz, *Reasonable Doubts: The O.J. Simpson Case and the Criminal Justice System* (New York: Simon and Schuster, 1996), 196–199.

## Epilogue: The Future of a Nation of Laws

1. James Madison, Federalist No. 10, *The Federalist Papers* (New York: Penguin, 1987), 127.

2. Morris Dees, with Steve Fiffer, *A Lawyer's Journey: The Morris Dees Story* (Chicago: American Bar Association, 2001), 348.

## The Sources of American Legal History

1. Rebecca E. Zeitlow, *Enforcing Equality: Congress, the Constitution, and the Protection of Individual Rights* (New York: New York University Press, 2006), 11.

2. Alan Watson, *Failure of the Legal Imagination* (Philadelphia: University of Pennsylvania Press, 1987), 107; Bernard Schwartz, *The Law in America: A History* (New York: McGraw-Hill, 1974), vii.

3. Karl N. Llewellyn, *The Common Law Tradition: Deciding Appeals* (Boston: Little, Brown, 1960), 36.

4. Lawrence Friedman, *American Law in the 20th Century* (New Haven, Conn.: Yale University Press, 2002), ix, xii; Friedman, "Introduction," in *The Law and Society Reader*, ed. Lawrence M. Friedman, Stuart MacAulay, and John M. Stookey (New York: Norton, 1995), 2.

5. Lawrence Friedman, *Dead Hands: A Social History of Wills, Trusts, and Inheritance Law* (Stanford, Calif.: Stanford University Press, 2009), 3–4.

6. Lawrence Friedman to the author, July 27, 2009; G. Edward White, *American Judicial Tradition*, 3rd ed. (New York: Oxford University Press, 2007), xx.

7. Roscoe Pound, "My Philosophy of Law" (1941), in Clarence Morris, ed., *The Great Legal Philosophers* (Philadelphia: University of Pennsylvania Press, 1970), 532; Richard Quinney, *Critique of Legal Order: Crime Control in Capitalist Society* (Boston: Little, Brown, 1974), 98.

8. James Willard Hurst, "The Law in United States History" (1960), excerpted in *American Law and the Constitutional Order: Histor-*

*ical Perspectives*, ed. Lawrence M. Friedman and Harry N. Scheiber (Cambridge, Mass.: Harvard University Press, 1978), 4, 5.

9. William E. Nelson, *The Legalist Reformation: Law, Politics, and Ideology in New York, 1920–1980* (Chapel Hill: University of North Carolina Press, 2001), 8.

10. Ann Curthoys, Ann Genovese, and Alex Reilly, *Rights and Redemption: History, Law, and Indigenous People* (Seattle: University of Washington Press, 2008), 16. A less-than-friendly view of the mangling of history in the service of constitutional argument is Martin S. Flaherty, "History 'Lite' in Modern American Constitutionalism," *Columbia Law Review* 95 (1995), 523–590.

11. On the justice and the professor, see Leonard Levy, *The Emergence of a Free Press* (New York: Oxford University Press, 1985), xvii–xviii. For a more sympathetic version of the possibilities of judicial use of history, see William E. Nelson, "History and Neutrality in Constitutional Adjudication," *University of Virginia Law Review* 72 (1986), 1237–1296.

12. The quotation from Kousser on expert witnessing is from Peter Charles Hoffer, *Past Imperfect* (New York: PublicAffairs, 2004), 124–127; the Kelly and Rothman quotations are from Curthoys, Genovese, and Reilly, *Rights*, 19, 16.

13. Elizabeth Mensch, "The History of Mainstream Legal Thought," in David Kairys, ed., *The Politics of Law: An Intellectual Critique*, 3rd ed. (New York: Basic Books, 1997), 1, 2.

14. Herbert Butterfield, *The Whig Interpretation of History* (New York: Norton, 1965), 39–40: oversimplified, moralistic, and inevitable rise of whatever party or ideology the historian favors.

# Further Reading

The literature of American legal history is immense. No list for further reading could do it full justice. Any published list would soon be out of date. Some of it is, to be sure, highly technical, but much of it is perfectly easy to follow. Here are some good choices for general works and reference works:

Benedict, Michael Les, *The Blessings of Liberty: A Concise History of the Constitution of the United States*, 2nd ed. (Boston: Houghton Mifflin, 2005). An excellent, concise survey of cases, personalities, and events in constitutional history.

Botein, Stephen, *Early American Law and Society* (New York: Knopf, 1982). The first of a series of essays with documents on law and society, Botein's remarkable synthesis remains a classic.

Friedman, Lawrence, *A History of American Law*, 3rd ed. (New York: Simon and Schuster, 2006), the newest edition of a superb work of the law-and-society type, covering the vast diversity of content with verve and purpose. A shorter version is Friedman's *Law in America: A Short History* (New York: Modern Library, 2004). One should not miss, as well, his Pulitzer-Prize finalist, *American Law in the Twentieth Century* (New Haven, Conn.: Yale University Press, 2002).

Grossberg, Michael, and Christopher Tomlins, eds., *The Cambridge History of Law in America* (New York: Cambridge University Press, 2008, 3 vols.). An unsurpassed and massive compendium of short essays on substantive topics by a wide variety of scholars and law pro-

fessors. The bibliographic essays alone are (almost) worth the price of
the volumes.

Hall, Kermit, et al., eds., *The Oxford Companion to the Supreme Court
of the United States*, 2nd ed. (New York: Oxford University Press, 2005).
The second edition of a very fine encyclopedic work. Essays range in
length from a few hundred words to ten thousand and are balanced in
perspective.

Hall, *The Magic Mirror*, 3rd ed. (New York: Oxford University
Press, 2007). A rival volume to Friedman's, with more emphasis on
institutions.

Hoffer, Peter Charles, Williamjames Hull Hoffer, and N. E. H. Hull,
*The Supreme Court: An Essential History* (Lawrence: University Press of
Kansas, 2007). A concise history of the Court, placing the lives of the
justices and their most important decisions in the context of their
times.

Katz, Stanley N., ed., The Oliver Wendell Holmes Jr. Devise *History
of the Supreme Court*, with volumes formerly published by Macmillan,
now published by Cambridge University Press. This superb series of
very large volumes has a history of its own. Justice Felix Frankfurter
entrusted his beloved mentor's funds to a select group of scholars,
largely Harvard Law School–trained. The result has been well worth
the wait. Published first in the 1950s and not yet done, the titles in this
series thus far are Alexander M. Bickel and Benno C. Schmidt Jr., *Volume 9, The Judiciary and Responsible Government, 1910–1921*; Charles Fairman, *Volumes 6–7: Reconstruction and Reunion, 1864–1888*; Owen M. Fiss,
*Volume 8: Troubled Beginnings of the Modern State, 1888–1910*; Julius
Goebel, *Volume 1: Antecedents and Beginnings to 1801*; Carl B. Swisher,
*Volume 5: The Taney Period, 1836–64*; George Lee Haskins and Herbert
A. Johnson, *Volume 2: Foundations of Power: John Marshall, 1801–15*; G.
Edward White, *Volumes 3–4: The Marshall Court and Cultural Change,
1815–35*; and William M. Wiecek, *Volume 12: The Birth of the Modern Constitution: The United States Supreme Court, 1941–1953*.

Kelly, Alfred H., Herman Belz, and Winifred A. Harbison, *The
American Constitution, Its Origins and Development*, 7th ed. (New York:
Norton, 1991). An alternative to Benedict, with a less balanced tone
after Belz took over from the deceased Kelly and Harbison.

White, G. Edward, *The American Judicial Tradition: Profiles of Leading American Judges* (New York: Oxford University Press, 2007). The latest and largest edition of this classic work on the nation's leading jurists. Judicial biography sometimes lionizes its subjects. White's assessments are clear, intelligent, and balanced. White's biographies of Earl Warren and Oliver Wendell Holmes Jr. are excellent as well.

Many legal histories focus on special topics. The following are some of the books that served as background for the accounts in the text, in addition to those works cited in the notes:

On lynch law and vigilantes, see W. Fitzhugh Brundage, *Lynching in the New South: Georgia and Virginia, 1880–1930* (Urbana: University of Illinois Press, 1993).

For the law of the Overland Trail, see John Philip Reid, *Law for the Elephant: Property and Social Behavior on the Overland Trail* (San Marino, Calif.: Huntington Library, 1980).

On regulation and the law, see Herbert Hovenkamp, *Enterprise and American Law, 1870–1930* (Cambridge, Mass.: Harvard University Press, 1991), and William Novak, *The People's Welfare: Law and Regulation in Nineteenth-Century America* (Chapel Hill: University of North Carolina Press, 1996).

On labor and the law, see Christopher Tomlins, *The State and the Unions: Labor Relations, Law, and the Organized Labor Movement in America, 1880–1960* (New York: Cambridge University Press, 1985).

For the debate over rights and "rights talk," see Akhil Reed Amar, *The Bill of Rights: Creation and Reconstruction* (New Haven, Conn.: Yale University Press, 1998).

The shift from instrumentalism to formalism is the cornerstone of Morton Horwitz, *The Transformation of American Law, 1780–1860* (Cambridge, Mass.: Harvard University Press, 1977).

On John Marshall, the classic anecdotal biography is Albert J. Beveridge, *The Life of John Marshall* (Boston: Houghton Mifflin, 1919, 4 vols.). More recent is R. Kent Newmyer, *John Marshall and the Heroic Age of the Supreme Court* (Baton Rouge: Louisiana State University Press, 2001).

On John W. Davis, see William H. Harbaugh, *Lawyer's Lawyer: The Life of John W. Davis* (New York: Oxford University Press, 1973).

On Clarence Darrow, in addition to his own *The Story of My Life* (New York: Scribners, 1932), see Kevin Tierney, *Darrow: A Biography* (New York: Crowell, 1979).

Two invaluable book-length essays on the legal profession are

Jerold S. Auerbach, *Unequal Justice: Lawyers and Social Change in Modern America* (New York: Oxford University Press, 1976), and Richard L. Abel, *American Lawyers* (New York: Oxford University Press, 1989).

On legal educators, see Robert B. Stevens, *Law School: Legal Education in America from the 1850s to the 1980s* (Chapel Hill: University of North Carolina Press, 1983), and N. E. H. Hull, *Roscoe Pound and Karl Llewellyn: Searching for an American Jurisprudence* (Chicago: University of Chicago Press, 1996).

On trials, see the volumes in the University Press of Kansas' Landmark Law Cases and American Society book series, edited by Peter Charles Hoffer and N. E. H. Hull. An online source of many primary materials for "Famous Trials," compiled by law professor Douglas Linder, includes the Salem cases, John Brown, the Susan B. Anthony trial, and the Scopes trial. The Web site is www.law .umkc.edu/faculty/projects/ftrials/ftrials.htm.

There is no complete guide to legal historical research. Legal research is a course in law school, sometimes called lawyering, for all first-year students. I recommend Morris L. Cohen and Kent C. Olson, *Legal Research in a Nutshell*, 9th ed. (St Paul, Minn.: Thompson, West, 2007).

One can find the primary sources of American public law on just about any subject easily enough. There are the professional online subscription sites like Lexis and Westlaw, and the free access Web sites like Yale's Avalon, FindLaw, and others. Libraries that are U.S. document repositories house the *U.S. Code Annotated*, the various versions of *Federal Rules of Procedure, Evidence*, and the like, and all the state codes and statute books. Alongside them stand reports of cases in the *U.S. Reports*, the official U.S. Supreme Court reporter, *West's Federal Cases* and *Federal Cases Supplements*, and all the state appellate court reports. These provide the original, documentary records of statutes, appeals court cases, and rules of practice. State legislative records and "file papers" are not as full as Congress's, and rarely do the state records include verbatim debates.

# Index